The Execution of Mary, Queen of Scots

Scottish Players and Plots

Stuart McCabe

Copyright@2019

Stuart McCabe has asserted his rights under the Copyright Designs and Patents Act 1988 to be identified as the author of this work

Cover design: The Execution of Mary Queen of Scots from a drawing by Sir John Gilbert (1817-1897). Background photograph by author.

To the good people of Ponfeigh. May the bridge over the dark waters finally be restored, and the buses to spin their wheels along the winding country roads below the mighty summit of old Tinto.

Stuart McCabe has survived a number of different types of employment throughout his life, many too tedious to mention, and others he would prefer to forget. Having a lifelong passion for history he decided to study several Open University subjects for the purpose of gaining a degree, which he did in 2014. Since then he has published several books on 16th Century Scottish history; *Let the Wolves Devour: War, religion and espionage during the Minority of Mary, Queen of Scots (1542-1560); Queen Margaret Tudor: The Story of a courageous but forgotten monarch*; *James, Earl of Moray: Sword of the Scottish Reformation*; plus works of Medieval and Hanoverian Scotland; and a horror fiction novella.

Contents

7	Introduction
9	The Captive Queen
31	The Minority of James VI of Scotland
35	Patrick, Master of Gray
51	Archibald, Parson of Douglas
63	The Babington Plot
72	The Trial of Mary
80	The Ambassadors
101	The Execution
108	After the Execution
114	The Fates of Gray and Douglas
126	Appendix: The Trial of Patrick, Master of Gray
131	Bibliography

The Execution of Mary , Queen of Scots

Introduction

Mary, Queen of Scots, mother of James VI of Scotland, the future King of England, was executed by beheading at Fotheringay Castle, Northamptonshire on February 8th, 1587. So died a rival to the rule of Queen Elizabeth I of England (1558-1603) and Mary's life would be expressed in legends and romances.

This book writes about the events leading to the execution, Mary's alleged involvement in an assassination plot against Elizabeth, the trial at Fotheringay, and the efforts of the Scottish ambassadors to save her life. It will examine the role of James VI, and the hidden agendas of two of the ambassadors; Patrick, Master of Gray, and Archibald, Parson of Douglas, both infamous intriguers, whose past adventures and endeavours had involved them many political plots, whether in the planning of rebellions, assassinations, blackmail, forgeries, and the toppling of governments.

The work will also look at the aftermath of the execution, the response of James VII, and his subsequent route to the throne of England which he would accept after Elizabeth died on March 24th, 1603.

The Execution of Mary , Queen of Scots

The Captive Queen

At 8 o'clock on the morning of February 8th, 1587, Mary, Queen of Scots was executed by beheading in the Great Hall of Fotheringay Palace in Northamptonshire, England. And so ended the life of one of the most controversial and romantic figures in British history. Aged just over forty-four years of age, her birthright as claimant to the English succession assigned her a central role in national and international conspiracies. And having lived nineteen years in England, she had been treated as a virtual prisoner, kept in close confinement by order of Elizabeth of England and her council. Her death would now release her from an existence that had swirled with religious struggle, political intrigue, warfare and violence.

Mary was born on 8 December 1542 at Linlithgow Palace, Scotland to King James V and his French bride Mary of Guise. Mary was the paternal granddaughter of Queen Margaret Tudor, who in turn was sister of King Henry VIII of England. Her father James would die soon after she was born, on December 14th at Falkland Palace, the cause uncertain although some claim some kind of physical and mental breakdown due to the defeat of a Scots army at Solway Moss. Before he died, the Calvinist preacher John Knox would have him state when he heard his wife had given birth to a girl, 'It cam wi' a lass and it will gang wi' a lass!' a reference to the legend of the Stuart dynasty which had began through the female line and was prophesized to be eventually lost by a female monarch.

Mary would be baptised at the Church of St Michael in Linlithgow, next to the Palace. Sir Ralph Sadler, the English diplomat would report that when he saw Mary in March 1543, 'it is as goodly a child as I have seen of her age, and as like to live.'

Mary was the rightful and lawful queen of Scotland, although she would have a number of half-brothers, illegitimate products of her father's promiscuous affairs with the wives of nobles and gentry. As she was an infant the government would be administered by appointed regents. This would result in power struggles between competing factions; one represented by Cardinal David Beaton who was also chancellor of Scotland. He rested his claim through a will supposedly written up by the dying king, although this would be dismissed as a forgery by his enemies. Beaton was powerful as he represented the church in Scotland, and had the backing of the Vatican as well as the King of France.

The other faction was lead by James Hamilton, 2nd Earl of Arran, who was designated second-person of the realm, or heir presumptive after Mary, since his grandfather James Hamilton, 1st Lord Hamilton (1398?-1479) had married Mary (1451-1488), daughter of King James II (1430-1460), and sister of King James III (1452-1488). Arran's claims were backed by many who were supporters of the Protestant reformation sweeping Europe, who were also in favour of a stronger alliance with Protestant England. Arran used a parliamentary session to take the position of Chancellor away from Beaton. He also won the support of any Scots Protestants captured at Solway Moss, many suspected to have sworn loyalty to Henry VIII in return for freedom. They would return to Scotland, the most powerful being the Red Douglas faction led by Archibald Douglas, the forfeited Earl of Angus, and his dangerous brother George Douglas. Archibald had been second husband of Margaret Tudor, and during a tempestuous separation leading to divorce, both Margaret and Archibald battled over possession of James V. Eventually

Margaret would win and Archibald and George were driven over the border to England, and her son James V would learn to rule as King of Scotland. Strangely enough, during this struggle Margaret's brother Henry sided with Archibald, and both he and George would receive English pensions during their exile. Archibald and Queen Margaret also had a daughter called Margaret, who Archibald would take to England. She would be raised in the English courts and become a favourite of her uncle Henry VIII.

A relatively young man born in 1519, Arran would by March 1543 become appointed Lord-Governor and tutor to the infant Mary. He would ensure that the forfeitures of many of the returning Scots were reversed in the parliament. He also introduced religious reforms and allowed the bible to be read in the vernacular, and there was the promise that he would seek to reform the state of the church for the benefit of the people. King Henry VIII of England would use the opportunity to propose marriage between Mary and his own son and heir, Edward, hoping for a union of Scotland and England. Arran supported this idea, and on July 1st 1543 the Treaty of Greenwich was signed, which promised that, at the age of ten, Mary would marry Edward and move to England. The two nations would remain legally separate and if the couple should fail to have children, the temporary union would dissolve. These negotiations had been done without the participation of Mary's mother Mary of Guise, who earlier in the year had been moved to Linlithgow, placed under restrictions by Arran's followers. For Arran, Mary of Guise and Cardinal Beaton were political rivals.

Cardinal Beaton had been briefly imprisoned, yet after regaining his independence at St Andrews Castle he worked to undermine the pro-

English treaty and to build up a Catholic revival backed by France. He began to push a pro-Catholic pro-French agenda. Matthew Stuart, Earl of Lennox would arrive around April in Dumbarton from France, as French ambassador and with an agenda to assist Mary and her mother. The Lennox-Stuarts were bitter rivals of the Hamiltons, Lennox's father John, 2nd Earl of Lennox had been murdered by the Hamiltons after the Battle of Linlithgow of 1526. Lennox as a youth had been financially exploited by the Hamiltons; eventually he would travel to France and become an officer in the Scots Guards where he gained some experience as a soldier. Beaton would promote the idea that Lennox was the rightful heir-presumptive after Mary, and this ploy worried Arran as there could be a case to say that his own claims were illegal as there was uncertainty about the legality of his father's divorce from his first wife Lady Elizabeth Home, which in turn challenged the legality of the marriage with his second wife Janet Beaton, Arran's mother, thereby questioning Arran's legitimacy.

Beaton's rise to prominence as the leader of a pro-French resistance angered Henry, who sought to break the Scottish alliance with France. There were fears that the infant-queen could be taken to England and Beaton wanted to move her away from Linlithgow to Stirling Castle. Arran sought to oppose Beaton's proposal and a battle came close to being fought at Linlithgow when both sides faced each other. Arran withdrew to Edinburgh as his forces were smaller, with Beaton able to command the support of four Earls, eight lords, twenty-three lairds and the Catholic Church. The Earl of Lennox would escort Mary and her mother to Stirling on 27 July 1543 with 3,500 armed men.

In Scotland there was growing anger to the terms of the marriage treaty, and Henry VIII made the matter worse when he had some Scottish merchants arrested who were set to sail for France. The Lord-Governor Arran could see that he was losing the political initiative in Scotland, and there was a threat that Beaton would engineer the raising of the Earl of Lennox as a rival Lord-Governor. The French were also expected to provide support, which was more appreciated by the people than the bullying attitude of Henry VIII. The Earl of Arran decided to change sides, and meeting Beaton at a Franciscan convent near Stirling he on September 8th renounced the Protestant faith and returned to the Catholic fold. Soon after, the infant-queen Mary was crowned in the Stirling castle chapel on 9 September 1543. Arran would be reconfirmed as Lord-Governor, as well as heir presumptive after Mary, and his son James would be placed into the custody of Cardinal Beaton in St Andrews.

In this political turnaround, the Earl of Lennox, who had hoped to become Lord-Governor and perhaps even marry the widowed Mary of Guise, reconsidered his options. He could not serve under his arch-enemy the Earl of Arran. Archibald Douglas, Earl of Angus and many of the Protestant faction wanted to continue the struggle against Cardinal Beaton, and continued their support for the Greenwich Treaty. Angus would propose a marriage treaty between Lennox and his own daughter Margaret Douglas. This would bring Lennox closer into the circle of Henry VIII and compensate for any loses from Scotland and France

The Treaty of Greenwich would be rejected by the Parliament of Scotland in December, which would follow with a renewing of the alliance with France. So began a war between England and Scotland termed the 'Rough Wooing', as the purpose was to convince the Scots to marry Mary to Edward, son of Henry. The English would partake in some devastating raids, by land and by sea. They also enjoyed the support of Henry's ally Charles V, the Habsburg Emperor, who loaned out foreign professional troops. In May 1544, the English Earl of Hertford invaded Edinburgh with fire and sword with Mary being taken to Dunkeld.

Cardinal Beaton would jointly rule Scotland with the Lord-Governor Arran; he was a competent statesman and soldier, taking part in several military expeditions. He was also a brutal oppressor of Protestants, his burning of the reformer George Wishart in 1546 would cause widespread anger. In May 1546, Beaton was murdered by Protestant lairds in St Andrews Castle which would lead a year long siege of Protestants within the castle, eventually broken by an armada of French ships. On 10 September 1547, nine months after the death of Henry VIII, the Scots suffered a heavy defeat at the Battle of Pinkie Cleugh. Mary was sent to Inchmahome Priory and the Scots would turn to the French for further assistance. Henry II, King of France proposed a union by uniting France and Scotland through the five-year old Mary marrying his three-year-old son, the Dauphin Francis. The Lord-Governor Arran would agree to the proposal when offered the French dukedom of Chastelherault.

In February 1548, Mary was relocated to Dumbarton Castle as the war became more destructive, the English gaining the town of Haddington, giving them a strategic foothold in Lothian. The arrival of a French fleet and army at Leith in June would lead to the siege of Haddington. Mary's mother would narrowly escape death when a cannonball blew away the church of St Margaret's in Haddington which she had been attending one Sunday. Several of her servants and gentlemen were killed. On 7 July 1548, a Scottish Parliament held at a nunnery in Haddington agreed to the French marriage treaty.

Mary was sent to France to spend the next thirteen years at the French court of Henry II sailing from Dumbarton on August 7th 1548 and arrived a week or more later at Roscoff or Saint-Pol-de-Léon in Brittany. She was accompanied by two of her illegitimate half-brothers, a governess Lady Janet Fleming, her father James V's half-sister, and four daughters of the families Beaton, Fleming, Livingston and Seton, called the 'four Maries'. Her mother would remain in Scotland and whilst Scots-French forces would eventually win the bitter struggle against England, she also fought a political battle against the Lord-Governor Arran

Mary's childhood at the French court was a happy period, where she was descried as beautiful, intelligent and full of life. She was a livid learner who became accomplished in music, able to play lute and keyboard instruments, as well as reciting prose and poetry. She enjoyed outdoor activities; falconry, horse riding, archery and hunting. She learned the arts and enjoyed a good education in science, religion, history and politics. She learned various languages and was able to speak and write in native Scots, French, Italian, Spanish and Greek. Her mother's Guise family ensured she would be protected and honoured; two of her uncles, Charles and Louis would become cardinals of Lorraine and Guise respectively, whilst her older uncle, Francis, Duke of Guise would win fame as a general. She was a popular figure at court except with King Henry's wife Catherine de Medici who saw her as a future rival. She grow fond of her future husband Francis, a awkward natured child, short in stature and with a stutter, and Henry II would comment when they both first met, 'my son and she got on as well together as if they had known each other for a long time.'

Mary possessed a long, graceful neck, pale skin, bright reddish-brown hair, light brown eyes, arched brows, a high forehead and oval-shaped head. As she grew into adulthood the pretty princess would be considered attractive, and tall, reaching a height of 5 ft 11 inches.

On April 4th 1558, Mary would be persuaded by Henry II to sign a secret undertaking where in the event of her dying without child she would devolve her claims to Scotland and England to the French crown. With this agreed on April 24th, Mary would marry the Dauphin Francis at the Notre Dame cathedral in Paris. There was now the possibility that the French king and the Guise family would gain a foothold into Scotland, leading to access to England. At that time Queen Mary, wife of Philip II of Spain was ruling England. Mary's mother Mary of Guise had gained the regency of Scotland in 1554 after James, Earl of Arran was persuaded to resign the position of Lord-Governor, although he would be assured of his French dukedom of Chastelherault. There had already been troubles on the Anglo-Scot borders, which was an offshoot of France's war with Spain, resulting in French troops based in Scotland pressurising the Scots to invade England. There was reluctance, many Scots were prepared to defend the borders but they did not want to fight for French interests, and this attitude was paralleled by many English who resented fighting for Spain. The complex politics emerging in Britain would change dramatically when on November Queen Mary would die and was succeeded by Henry VIII's only child, Elizabeth I of England, daughter of Anne Boleyn. Whilst the Third Succession Act of 1543 had ensured Elizabeth's rights to the crown, the Catholics in England considered that she was illegitimate, and that Mary Stuart, granddaughter of Queen Margaret Tudor of Scotland, and great granddaughter of Henry VII, was the rightful heir to England. Henry II would add to this controversy by declaring that Mary was Queen of England.

Within Scotland there was growing calls for religious reformation growing amongst ministers and clergy, inspired by men like Adam Wallace, burned for heresy in 1550, whose work was carried on by the likes of William Harlow, John Willock and John Knox. Support was offered by a section of nobility and gentry who would be termed the Lords of the Congregation, and in December 1557 they would produce manifestos and petitions for religious reform. The original members would write up a bond, signed by the Earls of Argyle, Glencairn, Morton, the Lord of Lorne, and Erskine of Dun. Their religion would develop toward a form of Calvinism, after the example of John Calvin of Geneva. During the spring of 1559 open hostility would ensue in Perth between Scots Protestants and Mary of Guise, backed by French troops. The hostilities would spread over a wider area, and the Scots Protestants would reach out to Elizabeth of England for help.

In 1559, with the prospect of peace between France and Spain, King Henry II was considering sending more French troops to Scotland in support of Mary of Guise a fact that would be a security concern for the fledging state of Elizabeth. Henry though would die on July 10th 1559 from a joust in Paris, resulting in Francis and Mary being declared King and Queen of France. Mary's relatives amongst the Guise family would become dominant powers in France and they were determined to secure Scotland with French power. Mary and Francis would also wear the arms of England, an insult and threat to Elizabeth.

By 1560 the Scots Protestants were fighting a desperate war against the French army of Mary of Guise. James Stuart, the Prior of St Andrews, and illegitimate son of James V, would enter the fray on the side of the

Protestants, but lacking money and arms they would invite England to intervene. Luckily the Scots had allies in the person of Lord William Cecil, secretary of state for England, who was also a personal friend of John Knox. The Treaty of Berwick would be agreed on February 27th, and an English army under the Duke of Norfolk would enter Scotland and join the Scots at Prestonpans on April 4th. The joint army would lay siege to Leith. The Scots were also helped by a Huguenot uprising in France, called the Tumult of Amboise, which in March 1560 made it difficult for the French to send any further support.

On June 11th 1560 Mary of Guise would die in Edinburgh Castle. The Guise brothers decided that a holding action was needed and sent representatives to Scotland, where in talks with their English counterparts the Treaty of Edinburgh was agreed on July 6th. France and England undertook to withdraw troops from Scotland, and France would recognise Elizabeth's right to rule England. When the treaty was brought to France, Mary and Francis would refuse to ratify it. The victorious Scots Protestants would establish a Reformation Parliament in Edinburgh on August 3rd. Papal authority and jurisdiction was abolished, and a confession of faith and doctrine was to be written up. The structure would be closely similar to that of the Calvinist churches of Switzerland and Huguenot France.

The French were still smarting over their failures in Scotland and there were rumours that King Francis was prepared to once more send French ships and troops across the seas. However King Francis II died on 5 December 1560, of a middle ear infection that led to an abscess in his brain. His other Catherine de' Medici, would become regent for the late king's ten-year-old brother Charles IX and next male successor to the throne. The devastated seventeen-year old Mary would be steadily pushed away from courtly influence and power.

After receiving an invitation from her half-brother James Stuart, prior of St Andrews, who travelled to France in 1561, Mary would return to Scotland in the summer arriving in Leith on 19 August 1561. The Catholic Mary, having spent her life in France since the age of five, had bravely placed herself into a country that was now fiercely Protestant. Scotland did not recognise the Catholic faith and had established hard laws against the practice of, yet under the protection of James Stuart she was allowed to tend to her faith in private. She would be faced with hostility and suspicion from the likes of the minister John Knox who would preach against her, against the Mass, and against her style of life.

Mary was a monarch who would involve herself in the day to day politics of Scotland, and she would be served by a privy council made up of up to 16 men, and a number of them would accompany her wherever she resided, whether Holyrood Palace in Edinburgh, or in travels across Scotland. Whilst Protestants dominated the Privy Council, there were four Catholics too powerful to persecute or prosecute; the Earls of Athol, Errol, Montrose and Huntley.

There would be a number of conspiracies that Mary would have to contend with early in her reign, one in the spring of 1562 involving James Hamilton, 3rd Earl of Arran, son of Duke Chastelherault, and James Hepburn, Earl of Bothwell, which would result in the former being locked up in Edinburgh castle apparently suffering a mental breakdown, with the former after a brief imprisonment escaping to France. Mary would also accompany an army into the Highlands in the autumn/winter 1562, to crush a rebellion by the Earl of Huntley.

Mary's main agenda was to be recognised as Elizabeth's heir in the English succession in the event of her dying childless. Elizabeth did however recognise the strength and validity of Mary's claim; however she would not name a successor as this could inspire Mary's supporters, of which she had many in England, to conspire against her. There had also been plans for both queens to meet at York or Nottingham in August/September 1562; this was cancelled due to warfare in France.

Whilst Mary felt herself shackled by the financial and religious restrictions of life in Scotland, she would consider that one route to better independence would be to marry. Her uncle Cardinal Charles of Lorraine had been negotiating for her marriage to Archduke Charles of Austria, this she rejected. There was also strong speculation that Don Carlos, son and successor of Philip II of Spain was one such prospect, although he was known to be unstable, and Philip himself objected. The possibility of a powerful Catholic in Scotland would concern Elizabeth and would be a threat to the stability of Protestant England. She would counter Mary's negotiations with European Catholics by offering Robert Dudley, 1st Earl of Leicester, a close friend of Elizabeth. Her half-brother James Stuart, now Earl of Moray, supported this match, although the negotiations would come to nothing. It be said that Leicester was not keen, and Mary was also concerned about rumours that Leicester and Elizabeth were lovers.

The next prospect was Henry Stuart, Lord Darnley, and son of Matthew Stuart, Earl of Lennox and Margaret Douglas, Countess of Lennox. Both mother and father were Catholics, and it was suspected that Darnley was also of that faith. He was also Mary's cousin, both being grandchildren of Queen Margaret Tudor, sister of Henry VIII of England. Mary and

Darnley would meet on February 17th, 1565 at Wemyss Castle. From that point on Darnley would win over Mary to the idea of marrying him. They married at Holyrood Palace on 29 July 1565. There was opposition, from James Stuart, Earl of Moray, who saw the match as a danger to the Protestant religion. Elizabeth, who had granted Darnley a licence to travel to Scotland, was outraged that an English subject of the royal line should marry without her permission. It also was dangerous, as both Mary and Darnley could muster support for their English claims from not just France, but also Spain and the Pope; both the latter would approve the match.

James Stuart, Earl of Moray would join with Chastelherault, the Earls of Argyll and Glencairn, and others in rebellion against the marriage. Mary would mobilise an army, and at Edinburgh on August 26th 1565 she begin a campaign, called the 'Chaseabout Raid', in which after several months of manoeuvring cross Scotland Moray would be pushed out of Scotland, crossing into England in October. This was a major victory for Mary; many of those that had defeated her mother had now been humbled. Mary had also invited the Earl of Bothwell back to Scotland, and released the successor Earl of Huntley from prison. More Catholics would be allowed into her privy council, and she was in contact with the pope and Philip of Spain, requesting support in the form of money. She would also learn that she was pregnant, with an expectation of birth for the summer of 1566.

Mary would also enter into a close working relationship with an Italian musician and singer called David Rizzio, whose knowledge of languages and administrative skills would win him a position of secretary to Mary. He would administer her crown lands, and would become the person that people would need to deal with if they were a tenant on those lands. It was said he became arrogant and would grow rich through bribery. There was also a report, written about by George Buchanan in his histories that Rizzio was preparing to engineer legislation for a parliament session on March 1566, where many of the exiled lords in England were to be forfeited. It was suspected that much of the legislation concerned with the reformation was to be reversed, French ambassadors, and letters from the Pope and Philip of Spain were pressurising Mary to restore the Catholic faith.

James Douglas, 4th Earl of Morton, was chancellor of Scotland and was tutor to the vast estates and titles of the Earldom of Angus on behalf of his nephew Archibald the 8th Earl. He had supported the marriage between Mary and Darnley, in return for Darnley's mother Margaret dropping any claims to the Earldom of Angus. Now there were fears that Morton would lose his position as chancellor, and that Darnley could rescind the deal regarding Angus. Morton set out to turn Darnley to his side by employing his cousin George Douglas, postulate of Arbroath and illegitimate son of Archibald, 6th Earl of Angus, to spread stories that David Rizzio was having an affair with Mary. By March 1566, Darnley and his father the Earl of Lennox would sign bonds with Protestants in Scotland, and with the exiled lords in England, to get rid of Rizzio who they accused of treason, and to grant Darnley the Crown matrimonial. In addition he agreed to preserve the Protestant religion, to pardon the exiled lords in England and welcome their return.

On 9 March, a group of the conspirators, accompanied by Darnley, murdered Rizzio in front of the pregnant Mary at a dinner party in Holyrood Palace. Over the next two days, the canny Mary who was practically placed under house-arrest, managed to convince Darnley to switch sides. Her half-brother Moray would also return with his fellow exiles. On the night of 11–12 March, Darnley and Mary escaped from Holyrood and rode to Dunbar Castle where they met with the Earl of Bothwell. Mary would return to Edinburgh with an armed force. Morton and his associates decided to leave for England, with Darnley having switched sides they had no political leverage and Morton suggested to Moray that he remain in Scotland and try to win pardons for these new exiles. Mary would pardon Moray and his friends, and they would once more become part of his council.

Mary's son James was born on June 19th, 1566 in Edinburgh Castle. However, the marriage with Darnley was filled with problems. Darnley felt he was steadily being alienated from the royal councils, the nobles did not trust him and he was loathed for the way he betrayed Morton and the rest. There was also talk that he planned to abduct his son and rule through him, or flee for the continent and condemn Mary with claims that James was not his son. At Craigmillar Castle during late November, Mary and leading nobles would gather and discuss options in regards to Darnley. During the course of the meeting there was a signing of what become known as the *Craigmiller Bond* by the Earls of Argyll, Bothwell, Huntley, Sir James Balfour and William Maitland of Lethington. Although the original does not survive there were copies that would present the following; 'It was thought expedient and most profitable for the common wealth ... that such a young fool and proud tyrant should not reign or bear rule over them; ... that he should be put off by one way or another; and whosoever should take the deed in hand or do it, they should defend.'

Darnley would learn of this bond and feared for his life. There were rumours that he would be arrested and during a feigned struggle he would be killed. He did not attend the baptism of his son at Stirling shortly before Christmas and travelled instead to Glasgow. He also suffered from an illness, either smallpox or syphilis, although poison would also be suspected.

In an apparent effort to reconcile their differences in January 1567 Mary invited Lord Darnley to stay with her in a house in Kirk o' Field, Edinburgh, where the fresh air could help him recover from his illness. On the night of 9–10 an explosion turned to rubble the house at Kirk o' Field, and Darnley was found dead in the garden, with no marks on his body although it would be later speculated that he was strangled.

The Earl of Bothwell was the chief suspect in the murder of Darnley, and the Earl of Lennox who had gathered evidence demanded that Bothwell be tried. A trial date would be set but Mary would steadily be accused of being a accomplice in the murder, and instead of arresting Bothwell she granted him offices and money, allowing him to raise a force of a estimated 4, 000 men to fill the streets of Edinburgh. Because of this large force, the Earl of Lennox, the principle accuser, did not attend the trial on April 12th. With no accuser and no evidence produced, Bothwell was acquitted after a seven hour trial on April 12th. Within a week Bothwell would arrange a gathering of lords and clerics at Ainslie Tavern, and filling them with food and drink, and surrounding the building with armed men he convinced the majority present to agree to support his new plan to marry Mary.

When Mary visited her son at Stirling, under the guardianship of the Earl of Mar, as she travelled to Edinburgh she was abducted by Bothwell on April 24th and taken to Dunbar Castle. He was alleged to have presented the Ainslie Bond, and when she did not immediately agree to the marriage he raped her. On May 15th Mary and Bothwell would go to Holyrood and were married in a Protestant ceremony. There would be widespread shock that Mary had married Bothwell, the man accused of murdering her husband. There is no doubt she was forced, that probably she believed her life was in danger, or maybe be was in a state of shock herself, the violence of the past few months taking a toll on her physical and mental strength.

Upon hearing of the rape, twenty-six Scottish peers, many who had also signed the Ainslie Bond, raised an army against Bothwell. They would become known as the Confederate Lords. The army of Mary and Bothwell would face the lords at Carberry Hill on June 15th, but there was no battle as Mary's forces began to fade away. During negotiations Bothwell was allowed to leave Carberry unhindered in return for Mary being placed under the protection of the Confederate Lords. However, as Mary was escorted to Edinburgh, crowds would gather and scream abuse and insults at her, accusing her of adultery and murder. After a night of captivity in Edinburgh she would be escorted to Loch Leven Castle, situated on an island in the middle of Loch Leven. This was the castle of the Earl of Moray's half-brother Sir William Douglas of Lochleven, and home of his mother Margaret Erskine who had been mistress of James V. There were attempts to persuade Mary to agree to divorcing Bothwell, and also of abdicating the crown in favour of her son James VI. She would refuse. It was rumoured she was pregnant and did not want to consign any child to illegitimacy if she divorced the father, who may have been Bothwell. Further pressure would be applied when the Confederate Lords managed to present material which they deemed as evidence of

Mary's involvement in the murder of Darnley, and evidence of an adulterous affair with Bothwell, said to have been discovered in a silver-gilt casket belonging to Bothwell. It contained love sonnets, unsigned love letters from Mary to Bothwell and two marriage contracts. Whilst this material which would become known as the *Casket Letters*, later condemned as forgeries by Mary's supporters, the Confederate Lords were prepared to use them as the basis of putting Mary to trial. The better option would be for her to abdicate and avoid such a trial. It was also said that Mary suffered a miscarriage of twins between July 20th and 23rd. She would be persuaded on July 24th to agree to abdicate the crown in favour of her infant son James VI. Her brother Moray, who was in France, would be offered the role of Regent of Scotland during James's minority. Initially she also refused to agree to divorce Bothwell, who would flee to Denmark and end up being imprisoned by the Danish King.

The coronation of James VI would occur at Stirling on July 29th with Morton taking the oath for the infant and john Knox giving sermon. Moray would arrive in Scotland on August 11th and accept the post of Regent of Scotland on August 22nd. From then on Moray would seek to establish control of Scotland, and also solidify the establishment of the Church of Scotland. Mary was kept in confinement at Loch Leven, allowed to use the grounds of the island but no further freedom of movement. Elizabeth of England was said to have been sympathetic to the plight of Mary, no doubt fearful of this dangerous precedent of subjects dethroning lawful monarchs.

Mary however was not without local or national supporters and on May 2nd 1568 she escaped from Loch Leven Castle. Reaching Hamilton she quickly managed to raise an army of 6,000 men. This army would face

Moray's smaller army at the Battle of Langside on May 13th where she was defeated. She had the option to find refuge in Dumbarton Castle and await a second army; instead she fled south, spending a night at Dundrennan Abbey then crossing the Solway Firth into England by fishing boat on May 16th.

After landing at Workington in Cumberland in the north of England and staying overnight at Workington Hall, she was then met by local officers and escorted to Carlisle Castle on May 18th. Mary appeared to believe that Elizabeth would support her regaining her throne, of which she would claim to have abdicated under duress. However Elizabeth realised she had a dangerous competitor in her throne, someone who could rely on the support of English Catholics as well as Protestants. She was placed under close confinement, and although Elizabeth would claim she was being protected she would be guarded night and day. Elizabeth decided to follow a middle course and raised an inquiry into the actions of the Confederate Lords, and also to raise the question on whether Mary was guilty of Darnley's murder.

In mid-July 1568 Mary was moved to Bolton Castle. A conference was held in York and later Westminster between October 1568 and January 1569. The Regent Moray and a group of supporters would attend this conference, as would representatives of Mary who would argue that the actions of the Confederate Lords were unlawful. Moray would produce the casket letters to justify the case for forcing Mary's abdication and changing the government. After studying the casket letters and comparing to the handwriting of Mary, the English commissioners would conclude that they were genuine. Elizabeth would not make a definite verdict, instead she consigned Mary to a type of legal limbo where the case against her was not proven and neither was the case against the Confederate Lords. Elizabeth decided to keep Mary in England until some solution was negotiated with the Confederate Lords, although this was difficult as there was a civil war ensuing in Scotland between supporters of James VI and those of Mary. Both factions would become known as King's Men and Queen's Men.

There were obvious dangers in regards to the status of Mary, if returned to Scotland she could regain her throne through French help, and next turn her ere on England. Or if Elizabeth allowed Mary to travel to France she could return with a French armada. On January 26th 1569, Mary would be moved to Tutbury Castle and placed in the custody of the Earl of Shrewsbury. Over the years Mary would be moved around the properties belonging to Shrewsbury; Sheffield Castle, Sheffield Manor Lodge, Wingfield Manor and Chatsworth House. Mary was allowed domestic staff of around sixteen, and she was kept in some relative comfort and style wherever she was housed.

Conspiracies would swirl around Mary; one Spanish project involved the Duke of Norfolk and a rebellion of northern Earls and Lords during the winter of 1569/70, which was successfully put down with support from Moray. Her brother would be assassinated in Linlithgow on January 22nd and a bitter civil war would pit Queen's Men against King's Men. Elizabeth realised that Mary was too dangerous and in 1571, Lord William Cecil and Francis Walsingham discovered the Ridolfi Plot, where Spanish troops with the aid of Norfolk would help replace Elizabeth on the throne with Mary. Norfolk was tried for treason and executed. The English Parliament would pass an act excluding Mary from the throne, and anti-Mary pamphlets were produced in England including copies of the Casket Letters.

There were several other plots; one was supported by Pope Gregory XIII in the late 1570s where Mary would marry John of Austria, half-brother of Philip II, and the governor of the Spanish Netherlands. The plan was for John of Austria to invade England from the ports of the Netherlands. There was also a plot in 1583 involving a former English envoy Throckmorton. Francis Walsingham would introduce *the Bond of Association and the Act for the Queen's Safety*, which gave legal sanction for the killing of anyone who plotted to kill Queen Elizabeth.

In 1584, to lift the restrictions of her confinement, Mary would offer her own idea of an *Association* with her son, James, which would be in the form of a joint rule of Scotland although she would be prepared to retire from politics and possibly remain in England. She was prepared to reject the Pope's bull of excommunication which had been raised against Elizabeth, and to abandon her own claims to the English Crown. She also offered to turn away from alliance with France and offer an offensive league with England. Further there would be a general amnesty in Scotland, no change in national religion, and an agreement that James would marry with Elizabeth's knowledge. Her only condition was the immediate alleviation of the conditions of her captivity. Whilst her son would consider the proposals, as did Elizabeth, both would reject it for there own negotiated treaty.

Mary could see no hope for release, and further plots would ensue in her name although not always with her knowledge. However one of her agents in France, Thomas Morgan was accused of being involved in another assassination plot, which in February 1585 would lead to the conviction of William Parry. There was no direct links to Mary only circumstantial evidence, yet in April Mary would be transferred to the custody of Sir Amias Paulet a much stricter custodian. By Christmas she was moved to a moated manor house at Chartley.

The Minority of James VI

James VI, king of Scotland was born at Edinburgh on June 19th, 1566, the son of Mary, Queen of Scots, and her husband, Henry Stuart, Lord Darnley. Following his father's murder, and his mother's enforced abdication, James was crowned as King of Scots on July 29th 1567 at the tender age of thirteen months with John Knox reading the sermon and James Douglas, 4th Earl of Morton taking the oath. During his early years James would be raised in Stirling Castle, where he would be baptised on December 17th 1566. John Erskine, 1st Earl of Mar and Annabella Murray, Countess of Mar would be appointed his guardians. During the minority of James, Scotland was engulfed in civil war, with James's supporters called the King's Men, and those of his mother the Queen's Men. Three of James's regents would die whilst serving in that post; Moray his uncle gunned down on the streets of Linlithgow in January 1570, his grandfather the Earl of Lennox murdered in Stirling on September 1571, and the Earl of Mar would die suddenly on October 28th, 1572. The war would end in May 29th, 1573 with the fall of Edinburgh Castle, the victor the fourth regent of Scotland, James Douglas, 4th Earl of Morton.

King James was highly educated; he received tuition by the scholar, humanist and historian George Buchanan. James became immersed in the arts, a good writer, and speaker with a wide grasp of philosophy. Whilst Scotland was a fiercely Protestant nation of a Calvinist structure, James was not prejudiced against other religions, and would tolerate the Catholic beliefs of some of his more powerful nobles, something that would anger and frustrate the church.

The nature of Scottish politics was at time complex, due to religion and the power structures where Scottish earls could amass vast power through lands and estates. James was in his earliest years shielded from the worst excesses of the political battles, until reaching the age of twelve in 1578 he would be asked to intervene in a dispute between the Regent Morton, and the Earls of Athol and Argyll. Morton would resent this intervention and offered his resignation, and perhaps hoping that James would back down, instead James accepted. The post of regent was no longer needed as James was prepared to allow the Privy Council to administer on his behalf; nevertheless the humbled Morton would dust himself off and soon intrigued his return to power through engineering a counter-coup at Stirling Castle.

James would in 1580, aged fourteen years of age, make the acquaintance of Esme Stuart, Sieur d'Aubigny, a thirty-seven year old cousin of the late Lord Darnley. Esme was a Frenchman, educated in renaissance France, cultured and learned, with also knowledge of the military arts having served in Flanders. James was enamoured by Esme when he arrived in Scotland, and whilst there is speculation about the exact nature of their relationship it may be James treated Esme as a surrogate brother or even father, someone he could admire and learn from. Esme was not trusted by the church or any of the stricter Calvinist nobility and gentry, with rumours that he was a papal agent out to undermine the Protestant reformation in Scotland. James however would reward Esme with offices and titles, one being the Dukedom of Lennox. Esme would also declare that he was converting to the Protestant religion; this though was greeted by distrust.

Esme would also befriend Captain James Stuart, a mercenary soldier and an individual brave and ruthless enough to challenge the Earl of Morton. He was son of Andrew Stuart, Lord Ochitree. During a Privy Council meeting Captain Stuart would on December 31st 1580 accuse Morton of being involved in the murder of Lord Darnley. Morton was arrested and placed in Edinburgh Castle and later Dumbarton. On June 2nd 1581 he would be executed in Edinburgh. Captain Stuart would later be made Earl of Arran by King James. With Morton out the way, and Esme gaining ascendancy in court, there were efforts instigated by Esme, which may have been his own secret agenda, to consider negotiating for the release of James's mother and her return to Scotland, with the possibility of establishing a joint-rule.

However, such was the nature of Scottish politics that new forces would arise to challenge the established powers. On August 1582 whilst out riding near Perthshire he met with William Ruthven, 1st Earl of Gowrie, and was offered the hospitality of Ruthven Castle. It was a trap, once spending a night at Ruthven, the following morning he was stopped from leaving. In what would become known as the Ruthven Raid, the coup would result in the fall of both the Earl of Arran who would be imprisoned, and the exile of Esme Stuart, of whom James was forced to write proclamations ordering him to leave the country, although in his duplicitous manner James would also smuggle out notes of assurance to Esme requesting his assistance in freeing him from Gowrie. Esme would eventually leave Scotland in December 1582. He would die in France on May 26th, 1583, declaring on his deathbed that he was still a Protestant.

James would escape from his captors in June 1583, where he rode to safety in St Andrews. The following day he was met by the Earls of Huntley, Crawford, Montrose, Rothes and the Earl Marshal, who would provide resources to counter the Ruthven Raiders. The Earl of Arran would return to court in August and dominate for the next few years.

A conspiracy by the Earls of Angus, Mar and the Master of Glamis was defeated in 1584, the conspirators driven into exile in England and given protection there. Andrew Melville, the firebrand minister would also flee across the border, accused of treasonous words against Mary. The Earl of Gowrie would be executed in Stirling on May 2nd, 1584, found guilty of treason.

Patrick, Master of Gray

Patrick, Master of Gray (1558-1611) was the son of Patrick, 5th Lord Gray, and Barbara, daughter of William Ruthven, Lord Ruthven. He was educated at St Andrews University, where he was said to be a committed Protestant. He would marry in 1575 Elizabeth, second daughter of John Lyon, Lord Glamis. The marriage was not a success, and they would later divorce in 1585 with Gray found to have committed adultery. From around 1575/76 the Master of Gray would live in France, where he associated with the likes of James Beaton, former archbishop of Glasgow and Mary's recognised ambassador in Paris. He was also friends with the Guise family and despite being brought up in Scotland a professed Protestant, in France he was suspected as a Catholic and supporter of the cause of the Marian party. He would correspond on behalf of the Guises with Mary and her supporters in Scotland, England and France, and would learn Mary's secrets and her many support networks. He would also win the friendship of the Spanish ambassador, and on a later date reportedly earn a reward for unspecified services, in the form of 'a cupboard of plate worth five or six thousand crowns'. No doubt Gray as a young man displayed enough personal charm and abilities to win over some of the most accomplished intriguers. His exact religion was unknown, and it was said that only his later patron the Earl of Leicester knew his leanings in this subject. This ambiguity would serve him as it allowed him to switch between Catholic and Protestant powers, whereas he could claim to be a secret Catholic to the French, seeking to work for Catholic interests in Scotland and England, whilst claiming to the English that he was using this mask to infiltrate Catholic networks so as to undermine them for the Protestant cause. He would become a remarkable double and sometime treble agent.

Gray would occasionally visit Scotland, and after the fall of Morton and the ascendancy of Esme Stuart during the summer of 1581, the church challenged Gray on whether he was a true Protestant. He was expected to present himself and renounce the Catholic religion, instead he returned to France. There he would remain until November 1583 soon after James had escaped the Ruthven raiders. His mission was to bring Ludovic Stuart, the son and successor of the late Duke of Lennox to Scotland. He and Ludovic arrived at Leith 1584 to be met by the Earls of Arran and Huntley, and there escorted to the court held at Kinneil. James would greet Ludovic with warmth and affection, and grant him the estates and titles held by his father. Gray would use the opportunity of this success to betray secrets of both Mary and the Guises to both James and Arran. During that period there were discussions which had begun by Mary, in which both she and James formed an *Association*, or joint rule of Scotland. In return Mary would renounce the Pope's bull of excommunication against Elizabeth; she would drop her claims to the English Crown and even offered to join an offensive league against France. In Scotland she agreed that the religion would stay unchanged. James and Elizabeth seemingly toyed with the idea, yet neither was serious, and much of the diplomacy involved in this proposal was to deceive the French and Spanish. The Master of Gray would be retained at court and would become a link between James and Mary, and his skill at intrigue would win the favour of the powerful James Stuart, Earl of Arran.

Gray would soon after come to the attention of the English. After a near five-hour long conference between the Earl of Arran and Lord Hunsdon at Founden Kirk on August 14th, 1584, the conclusion of what outwardly settled some severe disputes between Scotland and England, Arran introduced the Master of Gray to Lord Hunsdon as 'very young, but wise and discrete' who presented a letter of commendation from James and a request for a safe-conduct as he was to be sent to England as ambassador. In a private conference with Lord Hunsdon Gray would admit that besides any public business he had a secret agenda to reveal to Elizabeth the machinations of Mary, and this was to be done with the secret approval of James and Arran.

Whilst the Master of Gray was favoured by the Earl of Arran he would become fearful of his vindictive and destructive nature. Following the conference at Founden Kirk, Arran became aware of a plot by a number of lords who were exiled out of Scotland, to capture Edinburgh Castle. Arran ensured that he was appointed governor of the Castle and replaced the crown officials with his own people, and appropriated the royal residences for his own use. A parliament was called with bills of attainder being passed against around sixty people whilst exemptions were purchased by large amounts of money. Arran was not averse to public displays of his cruelty, when the widow of the Earl of Gowrie managed to approach the King in the street as he led a procession, and on her knees pleaded for herself and her children, Arran dragged James roughly away causing the widow to collapse and pass out.

There was also an attempt by Arran to get rid of enemies through assassination. In the north of England were based the exiled lords, the earls of Angus, Mar, the Master of Glamis, and others who had fled Scotland after the failure of the April 1584 conspiracy. They were favoured by Francis Walsingham the English secretary, and Elizabeth used their presence as a psychological lever against the Scots government. They longed to return to Scotland and enact revenge against Arran, Elizabeth however would not give them permission to cross or grant them money for this purpose. Nevertheless the Earl of Arran dreaded the return of the exiles and through the assistance of the Earl of Montrose recruited one of his clan, Jock Graham of Peatree. This Graham who was a borderer was housed in Edinburgh during the parliament and then brought to Falkland Palace. He would have a private meeting in the King's Gallery with Arran and Montrose, and later the King would join them. He was asked to kill the Earl of Mar, the abbot of Cambuskenneth and the Earl of Angus. Of the first two Graham declined as he had no grudge against them; however he had a blood feud against Angus and agreed to make an attempt against him, with an offer of sixty French crowns from the king and twenty pounds of land near Montrose. The Earl of Montrose gave Graham a matchlock, and suggested that he make the attempt against Angus at Newcastle where he was mostly residing. He also provided details that Angus could be surprised whilst walked on the beach or quayside, or whenever entering the church, or sitting at a table where he could be shot through door or window. Graham would travel to England however he was captured by the English and examined at Carlisle by Lord Scrope the warden of the western march. Francis Walsingham was informed of the results of the examination and around December informed the Earl of Angus and Earl of Mar, whilst keeping the information a secret from the public. It is tempting to speculate if the Master of Gray passed on this information about the assassination plot to the English authorities, which would have won him favour with the exiled lords.

The French ambassador Michel de Castelnau, Sieur de la Mauvissiere had developed suspicions about the Master of Gray, especially when learning that he was to act as James's ambassador. One of Mary's envoys M. de Fontenay, recently arriving in Scotland from France would communicate his own misgivings to his mistress. The Master of Gray would hear of these suspicions, which would have emerged once it was learned that he was to ask Elizabeth to withdraw from the plan where James and his mother are associated together. He would write to Mary before leaving Scotland, insisting he was still loyal whilst also stating that separating the cause of Mary from James was a temporary measure, and once the negotiations over James's claims were met then they would return to her rights. Mary would during the autumn be moved to Wingfield where on October 1st 1584 she wrote to the Master stating that she was not supportive of any dropping of the association, even if temporary, believing that staying united strengthened the cause of both son and mother. She also in the letter revealed rumours that were spread about the Master that his purpose was to reveal incriminating information regarding hostile actions by Mary against Elizabeth. Mary would also add that she believed the Earl of Arran was the instigator behind this, as a means to prove his commitment to friendship with England.

Before passing into England the Master of Gray would be made a gentleman of the royal bedchamber on October 4th, and a master of the wardrobe on October 7th. He would have a secret meeting with Lord Hunsdon in Berwick, where he outlined his official mission. He was to demand the delivery of the exiled lords or their banishment from England. He would ask Elizabeth to break off the treaty with Mary regarding the association. He was to argue that Mary's liberty would threaten both James's crown and that of Elizabeth as she was firmly attached to the Catholic faith. Thirdly the Master was to suggest that Elizabeth allocate to James a pension to counter any such offers from France or Spain. Whilst this was the official business, the Master had his own plans and he revealed them to Lord Hunsdon. On his own initiative he was prepared to make secret proposals to Elizabeth. He would ask her to allow the exiled lords to enter Scotland as an armed force ready to challenge Arran; in return the Master of Gray would reveal all the conspiracies that the Marion party were organising against her, and also the involvement of Mary in these matters. Lord Hunsdon would write to Lord Burghley giving his full confidence in the new Scottish ambassador. The Master of Gray would arrive in London where he would meet with Lord Burghley. It was recommended that he should meet with Walsingham who was a supporter of the exiled lords, and such a meeting might raise suspicions about Gray's secret agenda.

The Master of Gray would meet Elizabeth at her court. He would present the official requests of James and Arran. Of the request for a pension, the Master spoke of the danger of an impoverished James turning to France with the backing from the Earl of Arran. The Master would also use the occasion to turn his fire against Arran, informing Elizabeth that his proclamations of friendship were not genuine, that he acted as a tyrant drawing the anger and hatred of many powerful men who would eventually seek his downfall. The Master of Gray understood that Arran had selected him as ambassador to separate him from the King, as Arran was said to be jealous of the favour he was gaining. As Elizabeth had few influential allies in Scotland the Master offered his services, and if

Elizabeth would support him in toppling Arran, he would work to win pardons for the exiled lords, that he would reveal all the schemes and conspiracies against Elizabeth that he was aware of, and he would work to establish a strong league of defence between Scotland and England. Elizabeth found the Master's secret proposals agreeable, although to displace Arran would take careful planning and patience. If successful Elizabeth would no longer need to play games with Mary, and the fear of armies from Spain and France landing in Scotland would be diminished through the return of the exiled lords.

The talks between the Master of Gray and Queen Elizabeth would continue throughout the winter, and he would also win the confidence of Robert Dudley, Earl of Leicester who like Elizabeth became impressed with this ambitious young man. Elsewhere Mary would become aware that the Master was negotiating in the name of James only and she had been omitted. Mary managed to successful appeal to the King of France to lobby Elizabeth to allow her secretary to enter into the talks along with the French ambassador Castelnau. On November 28th 1584 Nau offered a set of articles, in accordance with an association of Mary with James, that she enter into a league with Elizabeth, renounce any claims to the English throne, recognise Elizabeth's rights to the crown, and renounce any support for papal bulls proclaimed against the English queen. Other articles were included, offering a firm alliance and friendship with Elizabeth, although when presented to the English council they were practically discarded, all opting to follow the course outlined by the Master of Gray. By the beginning of the following year 1585, as a result of more plots against Elizabeth being uncovered, Mary would be moved from Wingfield to Tutbury in Staffordshire and placed under the custody of Sir Amias Paulet.

Mary would write to the Master on December 14th 1584, now convinced that James had now rejected the idea of association she asked the Master to steer her son back to that course. The Master however had now rising in Elizabeth's estimation and could safely discard the association as a diplomatic device. Elizabeth would also order the exiled lords away from the Scottish borders to convince James and Arran that she was prepared to diminish the threat of the lords who were becoming vocal in their intentions to cross the border in force. She sent the Master back to Scotland during January, and to dissimulate against the Earl of Arran she wrote him a letter praising the ambassador. The Master would be congratulated by both the king and Arran upon the success of the embassy, especially the withdrawal of the exiled lords away from the borders. Although it was not the banishment they sought it was a good first step. James would write to Elizabeth approving the work of the Master, and assuring her he had never accepted or agreed to a royal association of power with his mother. During February he would also write to Mary practically discarding the idea of association.

With the exiled lords not an immediate danger, the Earl of Arran began to follow his avaricious desire and defrauded and oppressed the wealth of those less strong, taking their estates, lands and titles. The Earl of Athol, Lord Home and Master of Cassilis were thrown into prison for standing up to Arran's extortions, and he also alienated his ally Maxwell, Earl of Morton when he demanded certain lands. Morton refused and Arran recruited the mortal enemies of the Maxwells, the Johnstons, resulting in a battle at Crawford Muir and the return to bloody skirmishing across south-east Scotland.

During this period the Master of Gray would slowly build up a body of supporters willing to go against Arran when the time was right. One such was Sir John Bellenden of Auchnoull, the justice-clerk and one of the highest criminal judges in Scotland. King James would send Bellenden on a embassy to Elizabeth with information in regards to further conspiracies of the exiled lords, however when they were invited to London to face these fresh accusations, once they had made their defences Bellenden would state that he was convinced of their innocence. In private he would meet with them and make plans on how to topple Arran and win their pardons.

Another ally of the Master of Gray was John Maitland of Thirlestane, brother of the late William of Lethington, of whom he had shared the rigours of being besieged within Edinburgh castle during the civil wars. After some years of imprisonment and confinement Maitland had been brought to court by Esme, Earl of Lennox and would rise in favour with King James due to his loyalty to his mother as well as his political skills. By February 17th, 1581 he was rehabilitated, and by April resumed his seat at the Court of Session. He would seek to reform the Court of Session in his favour by introducing allies and friends onto the benches. He was not well loved by the clergy as he had drafted the Black Acts in May 1584 which also drew the suspicions of Elizabeth. Politically he would gain by becoming appointed secretary of state on May 18th 1584, his forfeitures were reversed soon after and he was also knighted. He had married Jane Fleming, whose mother was sister of Lord John Hamilton. Maitland was one who favoured bringing Lord John back to Scotland, and as the Earl of Arran held the Hamilton estates this no doubt caused suspicions. Other allies of Gray reported to be part of the conspiracy against Arran, were Andrew Wood of Largo, the Comptroller, Walter Stuart, prior of Blantyre and keeper of the Privy Seal, and William Keith, master of the royal wardrobe.

In the summer of 1585 Elizabeth would send a new ambassador Sir Edward Wotten to replace the recalled Davison. Wotton brought James a gift of hounds and horses for the king. Wotton was a courtier who loved hunting, horse-racing and hawking; was proficient in several languages and foreign customs; enjoyed conversation and banter. These attributes would appeal to James; although Wotton was also gifted at political statecraft and under the cover of amusements and entertainment he would warn James about the dangers of a Catholic league amongst the European powers, and suggest that best protection was through alliance between Scotland and England. Wotton's instructions were to convince James to enter into an Anglo-Scot league; to offer the possibility of a pension although not give an amount; and to discuss the idea of a marriage, where either the Princess of Denmark or Arabella Stuart was considered. Wotton also pleaded for the return of the exiled lords who had recently passed examination by Bellenden. James would be impressed by Wotton's arguments regarding a closer league with England and would call a convention of nobles to meet at St Andrews to debate it.

Wotton was to work with the Master of Gray and Bellenden, these three Leicester would describe as his 'assured deputies' in a letter to Maitland. They were to instigate plans to rid Arran from court. Already there was an assassination plot which had been in progress when Wotton arrived in Scotland. Bellenden would secretly introduce to Wotton one of the prospective assassins. Wotton however would not support such a plan and it would soon after be uncovered.

Another opportunity to intrigue against Arran would arise during the summer. On July 28th 1585 at a meeting between English and Scottish wardens at the borders of Teviotdale between Sir John Foster and the Laird of Ferniehurst, a violent affray occurred between their followers, and Lord Francis Russell son of the Duke of Bedford, and son-in-law of Foster was killed by a pistol shot. There were several different accounts of the incident, nevertheless there was a danger of this developing into a major diplomatic breach between Scotland and England. The Master of Gray would spread a report that as Ferniehurst was one of Arran's allies that they both contrived at the death of Russell. Wotton with the encouragement of the Master of Gray would produce Foster's written account of the incident and demand the arrest of Arran and Ferniehurst. James concerned about English anger sought to appease them by having Arran placed in St Andrews Castle with the promise that he would be sent to England for trial, whilst Ferniehurst was placed in Dundee. Arran managed to send a letter to Maitland in which it was alleged that the killing of Lord Russell had been instigated by the exiled lords in London. It was also alleged by the church historian Calderwood that the Master of Gray then began to convince James to become more lenient with Arran, 'tickling in' the king's ear to 'let bygones be bygones, in fair play in time to come'. The Master's actions would perplex Elizabeth, Wotton and Walsingham. His reasoning is unclear although he may have perceived that James would not withdraw his support of Arran and would eventually have him released, so he decided to ensure that in the short term he was on Arran's side. There was also the matter of a large bribe which the Master accepted for taking Arran's side, something he admitted to Wotton, claiming his 'virtue' was not strong enough to resist. Wotton would advise his English masters to forgive this indiscretion. James would transfer Arran to ward in his own home at Kinneil, and 'began to deal with the Queen of England for Arran'. James also wanted Arran to remain as councillor in the Anglo-Scot league discussions.

The Master of Gray would also provide another reason for his change in direction, he wrote to the arch-schemer in London Archibald Douglas, believing himself in a perilous position that having pitted his wits against Arran he was now being deserted by Elizabeth. He outlined his options; clearly he could not trust Arran, despite having recently helped him he understood this would only provide a temporary halt to Arran's malice and treachery. He then suggested that Archibald try to persuade, the Douglass and the Hamiltons to join forces in preparation for crossing into Scotland. With this plan agreed Archibald would successfully get the Earl of Angus, the Earl of Mar, Lord Glamis and their allies to settle their differences with John Hamilton, Lord Arbroath and his adherents. The Master would make efforts that they be joined on the Scottish side by Francis Stuart, Earl of Bothwell, Archibald's stepson, and also Lord Hume and the laird of Cessnoch. He was also hopeful that the Earl of Morton would add his forces. Such an army would cause the King to yield or flee Scotland.

Soon the Master of Gray spoke to Wotton at a royal hunt around Dumbarton. He asked him to send word to Elizabeth and convinced her to delay the negotiations regarding the Anglo-Scot league, which through Wotton were close to agreement, and to also allow the exiled lords to return to Scotland. If they could be furnished with some money and crossed the border, the Master and his friends would secure the king and throw Arran in prison.

Whilst all the pieces were in readiness, Elizabeth hesitated. The Earl of Arran aware that there were forces gathering against him began to make contact with French agents and accept their money and promises of support. He was also in contact with three Jesuit priests and there was talk of restoring Mary and the Catholic faith to Scotland. He was also determined to crush the strongest opponent currently in Scotland, and convinced James to order a muster for Crawford Muir on October 24th 1585 to march against the Earl of Morton. Wotton would write to Walsingham on October 5th warning of this muster, Elizabeth realising that Morton was important to the success of any enterprise against Arran, gave permission for the exiled lords to cross into Scotland. Angus, Mar and Glamis made a show of thanks at Westminster where 'many tears were poured out before the Lord', then they joined with the exiled ministers Andrew Melville, Patrick Galloway and Walter Balcanquhal, and marched north joining with the Hamiltons at Berwick. Upon learning of the advance of the exiles James was aware that Wotton must have played a part. He ordered his arrest, planning to take him with the army which James intended to lead against the exiles. Wotton however managed to slip capture and ride a fast horse to Berwick.

The exiles crossed the border, met allies at Kelso, and then separated to raise more forces. By October 31st they rejoined at Falkirk with 8,000 men. The Master of Gray had been in Perthshire and Fifeshire raising men under the pretext that he intended marching with the king against Morton, although the true purpose was to use the forces assist the exiles. When Arran learned of the crossing of the exiles he broke his ward at Kinneil and rode to Stirling Castle to join the king. He also convinced James to summon the Master of Gray who he now suspected of being a prime mover in these happenings. The Master realising that if he refused the full conspiracy could be undone, decided to obey the summoning, and arriving at Stirling he convinced the king that he was innocent of Arran's suspicions. Arran and his friends decided that they would take matters into their own hands and kill the Master, even if in the king's presence. He was to be killed on November 2nd, fortunately for Gray the army that had mobilised at Falkirk had by that time advanced to within a mile of Stirling.

On November 2nd the invading army approached every entrance into the town, whilst the Earls of Arran and Montrose tried to mobilise a defence. Despite having the greater numbers the defenders were not as united or resolute as the attackers, and when the exiled lords issued orders to try and avoid unnecessary bloodshed some companies would switch sides. The Earl of Arran was guarding the bridge and the main attack began to concentrate on his position. Seeing little hope of success and fearful that capture would lead to his death, Arran locked the bridge, threw the keys in the river, took mount and with one attendant fled Stirling. The army of the exiled lords entered Stirling and those under the earl of Morton began to loot the town. Arran's allies the Earls of Crawford, Montrose and other nobles would join the king within Stirling Castle.

The castle was in no condition to sustain a siege through lack of victuals or strong defences. The king sent out the Master of Gray to parley with the besieging force and to ask the cause of their invasion. They replied that they wanted to enter the castle and to offer their submission and obedience to the king. After some back and forth negotiations it was agreed that the exiled lords could enter the castle on condition that they respect and honour the person of the king, and make no change or innovation of the government. On November 4th the castle gates were opened and the exiled lords entered. They made their submissions to the king who expressed pleasure that so little blood had been shed during their venture. The Earls of Crawford, Montrose, Rothes and others were arrested. The Earl of Arran was declared a traitor at the market cross and King James acceded to the request of the exiled lords, with John Hamilton, Lord Arbroath acting as spokesman. The following day a royal proclamation was produced where the king gave approval to the exiled lord's action, and forgave past crimes and actions, with pardons being granted. The master of Glamis was appointed captain of the guard, the laird of Coldingknowes was entrusted with Edinburgh castle, the Earl of Angus was granted Tantallon castle, the Earl of Mar Stirling castle and Lord Arbroath Dumbarton. The Master of Gray would along with John Maitland of Thirlestane write letters to Walsingham announcing the success of the revolution against Arran who had fled to the west coast. The Master had proved himself a great strategist and intriguer.

The success of this expedition prompted Elizabeth to send Sir William Knollys to Scotland and to continue negotiating the proposed league between Scotland and England. At Linlithgow on November 23rd 1585 James would express his friendship to Elizabeth and England, with a determination to resist the Catholic league. Early in December a parliament was called and an act was passed allowing the king to enter into a league with England and James addressed those assembled with his support for the establishing of a firm league of Protestant princes against the Catholic league. The Earl of Morton, who had been a principle agent in the success of the revolution, was also a practising Catholic. He would go to the college church of Lincluden and celebrate mass on the 24th, 25th and 26th of December 1585. For this crime he would be summoned before the Privy Council and jailed in the castle of Edinburgh. King James would follow this by producing a proclamation calling on all priests, Jesuits and sympathisers to leave the country under pain of death. Knollys doubted the King's sincerity, he would be aware that there was a party of Jesuits led by the energetic William Holt who were being protected in the north by the Catholic earls of Huntley, Crawford and Montrose, and other nobles.

Archibald, Parson of Douglas

With the success of the revolution against the Earl of Arran and James VI now veering towards alliance with England, Henry III of France was naturally concerned. Prior to the revolution the French king had been trying to send his London-based ambassador to Scotland for a short visit, only to be blocked by Elizabeth. Henry decided to send a more permanent ambassador to Scotland, choosing Baron d'Esteval, who would receive instructions on October 7th, 1585 to travel to the court of James. He carried letters from the King of France and the Queen-mother, offering friendship, with assurance that the recent revocation of religious liberty in France would not lead to violent oppression against Protestants, and any of the reformed religion were free to leave France with all their belongings. M. d'Esteval was also to learn if James had entered into any secret leagues with the French Huguenots. He was also to seek reconciliation between James and his mother. He also carried letters addressed to the principle nobility, proposing that they assist in renewing the old treaties between Scotland and France.

M. d'Esteval would be delayed in his travel to Scotland by the revolt against Arran, and it was only until early January that he managed to finally meet James. He was to make friends with the Hamiltons, especially John, Lord Arbroath, and also his brother Lord Claude who had been invited by James to return to Scotland and take over Dumbarton Castle, leaving France on January 31st 1586. Whilst James welcomed the new French ambassador, he also sent Sir William Keith of Delny to England to assure Elizabeth of his continued goodwill and with a request that she send another ambassador to Scotland, the previous ambassador Knollys had returned south. Keith was the illegitimate son of the Earl of Buchan, although this did not bar him from being appointed King's valet in 1579, and by 1583 he was known to enjoy his 'special favour'.

Thomas Randolph, the new English ambassador to Scotland, would arrive in Edinburgh on February 26th, 1586. Randolph had a wealth of experience in Scottish affairs and had been present at many of the key political events since the Reformation. James would remember that when Randolph was last in Scotland he fervently protested the arrest of James Douglas, Earl of Morton on December 1580, denounced the Duke of Lennox and fled after being implicated in a plot to capture the king. James would pragmatically welcome the ambassador with friendship and honour. Randolph would discover that Scotland was a busy place for foreign intrigue, not only was M. d'Esteval seeking to undermine English influence there were also agents of Mary in Edinburgh, as well as Jesuit spies led by Holt, who were being protected by Huntley and the Catholic lords. Randolph would demand the Holt and the Jesuits are either rounded up or expelled from Scotland. His prime objective was the forming of a league between Scotland and England based on defence of their religion. He was also to ask that the Earl of Morton is prosecuted for the recent masses taken at Lincluden, and for more vigorous actions to be made against the Earl of Arran who was in the west, and to demand that the laird of Ferniehurst is handed over to English authorities for his part in Lord Russell's killing.

James would insist during his initial audience with Randolph that he would proceed against the Maxwell Earl of Morton and against Jesuits within Scotland. Morton however would be released and the Jesuits would escape arrest. There was some hesitancy regarding the signing of the league, with the secretary Maitland and other nobles holding out for commercial privileges in England; and a proclamation on their king's right to the English succession; as well as a substantial pension. Randolph however would not give a figure for the annual sum of the pension that would be bestowed on James, although Wotten had apparently quoted a sum of 20,000 gold crowns. The French ambassador M. d'Esteval would also try to mobilise opposition amongst the Scots against the league, insisting that there was no threat to destroy the Protestant religion with the Catholic league and therefore no need for a Protestant league. The Scots Catholics in turn presented a plan to d'Esteval in which in return for French support they would take command of the King of Scotland's person and forestall any religious persecution against them. The conspirators would be named as the recently released Earl of Morton, Lord Claude Hamilton, the Earls of Huntley, Montrose and Crawford, and there were hopes of joining with the Earl of Arran lurking in the west. The King of France did not trust these conspirators, and also had not the money available to fund a rebellion. He would send word to his ambassador to ask them to stay quiet and play the loyal subjects to avoid persecution. James would be won over by Randolph's diplomacy during subsequent meetings and on April he would sign the league. Randolph's secretary Milles would travel to England with the signed treaty.

The League would be ratified at Berwick on July 31st, 1586 by commissioners of both countries including Thomas Randolph. It was a league of mutual aid in defence of religion. There were no commercial rights included, although it allowed that all Scots living in England would become naturalised subjects. There was no mention of James's succession rights, although it significantly made no mention of Mary. Later James would be offered 4,000 pounds as a yearly pension, lower than he expected although having already signed the league he could not appeal

M. D'Esteval would protest several times to James against the basis of the league, claiming that there was no Catholic design by the French king or others to oppress Protestants, only a sovereign right for Catholic princes to put down religious rebellions amongst their subjects. Henry III would also write seeking clarification on rumours that James was allowing Scottish troops to mobilise for travelling to France and fighting alongside Huguenots. Whilst Protestants would sign up to fight alongside co-religionists in France, d'Esteval did not gain any definite information, although he would warn James that any Scots raised to support Huguenots would be fighting against Scots allied with the Catholic king. M. d'Esteval would leave soon after the league was signed and travel to England leaving behind his secretary Courcelles. A Spanish report from England, dated August 8th, 1586, would claim that the pension paid to James would finance a guard who would naturally would be devoted to their paymaster Elizabeth, and thereby the king would be 'so to speak, her prisoner.'

Another one of Randolph's objectives when he arrived in Scotland was to win a pardon for Archibald Douglas, Parson of Douglas. This was done with the written approval of Elizabeth. Archibald was known as one of the most notorious conspirators of his day. Born in 1540 the son of William of Whittingham and Janet Matheson, he had an older brother William of whom he would be associated in several infamous escapades. This brother William would join the Lords of the Congregation during the struggle for reformation, and after being awarded the ecclesial lands of

Whittingham in August 1560 he would become employed as a representative of the General Assembly of Scotland, later acting on their behalf in business with Queen Mary and the Privy Council. Archibald was educated for the priesthood in France, graduating with a M.A. A early convert to the Protestant religion and expert in canon law, by June 1562 he would be appointed parson of St Bride's Church in Douglas, and custodian of the altar-tombs belonging to famous figures in Clan history, including the 'Good Sir James' Douglas, lieutenant of 'The Bruce'. He appears to have worked as a royal clerk, and in 1565 he was an extraordinary Lord of Session. By February 1566 he would be sub-dean of Orkney. Archibald was a participant in the murder of David Rizzio in March 1566, which was reportedly planned at the family castle of Whittingham. After Mary successfully escaped her captors the conspiracy was defeated and Archibald fled France where he found favour with King Charles IX. He would return to Scotland apparently with the support of Lord Darnley, and he successfully acted as a representative of the exiled lords, securing pardons for many of them on December 25th, 1566. He then switched sides and became an agent for Bothwell, participating in the murder of Lord Darnley in February 1567. According to the testimony of his own servant George Binning who was executed in June 1581, Archibald was present at the murder, and hurrying away from the scene, his clothes covered from clay, soil and dust from the explosion, he lost one of his slippers which he had used to muffle his footsteps. James Douglas, Earl of Morton, and the former regent of Scotland would be beheaded also in June 1581 for being 'art and part' in the murder of Lord Darnley. Hours before his execution in Edinburgh he informed two ministers that Archibald had tried to recruit him to participate in the murder which Morton refused. Morton would also claim that Archibald admitted of being alongside the Earl of Bothwell and Huntley during the murder. After the fall of the Earl of Bothwell in June 1567 and the imprisonment of Queen Mary in Lochleven Castle, Archibald would help secure the Casket Letters which would be used to incriminate Mary as a accomplice in the murder of Darnley, and he would be accused by later historians of being responsible for forging some of the letters and notes. On June 2nd 1568 would be appointed ordinary Lord of Session in place of John Leslie, Bishop of Ross.

Archibald would gain the parsonage of Glasgow in 1570 although he would not gain possession until January 23rd 1572 after some opposition from the General Assembly. It appears through his own admission and under examination by church authorities that he was not suitably skilled in the work of parson, or any good at delivering prayers. His abilities though were in the political arts.

Whilst there was wide belief that Archibald Douglas had been involved in Lord Darnley's murder, Darnley's father Matthew Stuart, Earl of Lennox, when regent, employed him as a ambassador to the Earl of Sussex in September 1570. It is tempting to speculate that Archibald had successfully traded away any possibly of facing Lennox's vengeance by giving details about the conspiracy. Lennox for example was well informed about the names of accomplices soon after the murder, and the casket letters reportedly located by Archibald Douglas helped sow doubt about Mary's innocence in the minds of the English commissioners and Elizabeth during the York/Westminster conferences. After the murder of Lennox, Archibald would continue to work with Morton. In April 1572 he would be accused of assisting with the smuggling of money and supplies from the Duke of Alva to the Queen's Party in Edinburgh Castle, valued at 4-5 thousand crowns, and would be locked up in Stirling Castle. He was also accused of plotting to kill Morton. William Drury, Marshall of Berwick would later claim that Archibald was being employed by the English to infiltrate the Marian networks and capture George, 5th Lord Seton, who was a prominent international agent for Mary. For this Archibald had received a pension from England. He would then be locked up in Lochleven Castle for a brief period; afterwards he would be released and seemingly allowed to live privately. Little is known about his activities from then until he married in 1577 Janet Hepburn the sister of James Hepburn, Earl of Bothwell and widow of John Stuart, abbot of Holyroodhouse and half-brother of Mary. This made him stepfather to Francis Stuart the later Earl of Bothwell. Janet was also widow of John Sinclair, Master of Caithness. By 1581 Janet would seek a divorce. Archibald would return to the bench on November 11th, 1578, apparently through a request from James VI, however he appears to have been overcome with a serious illness which prompted his brother William to stay by his side, and both would on January receive permission not to attend court. He would eventually recover and once more become associated with the Earl of Morton.

When Morton was arrested in December 1580, accused of being an accomplice in the murder of Darnley warrants were made out for Archibald who was in Morham, England. Thomas Randolph, the English ambassador to Scotland was quickly appointed in January 1581 to save Morton's life, and meeting refusals from the Scottish parliament entered into a conspiracy with the Earls of Angus and Mar to capture the King, and kill or capture Esme Stuart, Duke of Lennox. The plot would be uncovered and Archibald's brother William, laird of Whittingham would be arrested and threatened with the rack. He would reveal details of the plot and also gave the names of those servants of Morton who were involved. William also informed his interrogators that his brother Archibald had forged letters incriminating the Duke of Lennox in papal plots. Elizabeth would refuse to extradite Archibald from England when James VI demanded. Archibald's servant John Binning would be arrested and executed for his part in the murder of Lord Darnley and would reveal details of the involvement of his master. Morton would be executed on June 2nd 1581 and Binning the following day.

In England Archibald would become an agent for Francis Walsingham. Incredibly he won the confidence of the French ambassador Michel de Castelnau, Sieur de le Mauvissiere, making himself available to French intrigues. Castelnau would write to the Queen-mother Catherine de Medici of how he trusted in the faithfulness and ability of Archibald Douglas. This allowed Archibald to befriend his former enemy Esme Stuart, Duke of Lennox and play a part in the schemes of the French. However, Archibald would pass what information he gathered to his English friends. When after the Ruthven Raid of 1582, which put James in the power of the Protestants who were opposed to the Duke of Lennox and Earl of Arran, Archibald would write on September 12th to Thomas Randolph the former English ambassador to Scotland about affairs in Scotland. He had learned through his impressive network of contacts that the Earl of Arran was prepared to do a deal with the Ruthven Raiders, seeking to return to the King's favour in return for accusing Lennox of treason. Several days later letters from Archibald sent to Scotland would be intercepted and orders made for his arrest. He would be taken into custody and examined by Sir Henry Killigrew, and according to Castelnau no discoveries were made which convinced the French ambassador that Archibald was faithful. The arrest was a ploy for Archibald's house was searched and many letters and documents were found which incriminated Lennox in political plots. Through these discoveries Esme would be accused by the English authorities of plotting to subvert the Protestant religion; of being a agent in the papal designs of the Bishops of Ross and Glasgow; and of favouring a restoration to power of Mary by her entering into a political association with James. Such accusations made it difficult for Lennox to return to the Scottish court and he would sail from Dumbarton in late September and spend time on the Isle of Bute considering his next move. James would be persuaded to banish Lennox from Scotland, and Elizabeth allowed him safe passage to return to France. He would die in the summer of 1583 after a lingering illness.

After a spell of imprisonment, possibly a ruse to fool the French, Archibald would travel to France. From between April to November 1583 he would enter into communication with Mary and her agents, asking her to intercede on his behalf with James VI. Mary was so convinced that the talented and resourceful Archibald, her former enemy, could become a useful servant, and on November 12th, 1583 wrote to the French ambassador in London Michel de Castelnau, Sieur de le Mauvissiere stating she may help him in his request although she wanted to learn if he had been involved in the plot to kill Lord Darnley. Archibald would write to Mary, and whilst making no mention of the plot to kill Darnley he did admit that in 1566 he was a representative for those including himself who were exiled for the Rizzio murder.

Archibald would return to England around 1584 and he appears to have acted as an unofficial ambassador at the English court representing Scots in London. He was well known and close to several important individuals who supported continued friendship between England and Scotland, based on defence of the Protestant religion. He could count as friends the likes of William, Lord Burghley, and Lord Treasurer, who had played a decisive role during the Scottish Reformation of 1559/60, in supporting the Lords of the Congregation against the French forces of Mary of Guise. Burghley had been a close friend of John Knox and understood the Calvinist mindset of the Scots reformers. There was also Sir Thomas Randolph, the professional envoy and ambassador, who would act as link between Scotland and the English court. He had been a close friend of George Buchanan, as well as James Stuart, Earl of Moray, attending the latter's funeral. He was vigorous in defending James Douglas, Earl of Morton when he was arrested in 1581, and tried unsuccessfully with Archibald Douglas to arrange Morton's escape. There was Robert Dudley, Earl of Leicester, the intimate friend of Queen Elizabeth, and at one time a prospect for marriage with Queen Mary of Scotland. He in December 1585 had led an expedition of 6,000 Englishmen to the Netherlands in support of Dutch Protestants against the Spanish, and whilst not a good commander his support for the cause of religion had won the respect of many like minded Scots. Sir Francis Walsingham, Secretary of State, is widely attributed to establishing one of the best spy networks in Europe. His own fears of French or Spanish intervention in Scotland or England stemmed from his time in Paris during the St Bartholomew Massacre of August 1572, when thousands of Huguenots were slaughtered indiscriminately by the orders of the French King Charles IX.

Archibald Douglas would act as a link between the above influential Englishmen and any Scots seeking friendship or favour in England, especially the exiled lords led by the Earls of Angus and Mar, as well as the banished ministers led by Andrew Melville. As noted above he also played a part with the Master of Gray in the forging of an alliance between the Douglas and Hamilton clans which led to the downfall of Arran. He was also step-father to Francis Stuart, Earl of Bothwell which offered further sources of information in Scotland, as well as opportunities to intervene. French interference would be also minimised as the French ambassador Castelnau was recalled to France in the autumn of 1585 and it would only during the following autumn that a new French ambassador was appointed.

When Randolph presented Archibald Douglas to the young king of Scots in May 1586, James was faced with a fellow who had been involved in the slaying of Rizzio, was accused of being a participant in the slaying of his father Lord Darnley, had conspired against his friend Esme Stuart, Duke of Lennox, and had played a part in the latest coup against the Earl of Arran. Whilst it would be understandable if James showed no favour to a man of such infamous reputation, yet Elizabeth would vouch for Archibald's return by letter which James graciously received. Not just Thomas Randolph would intercede on Archibald's behalf, there would also be members of the nobility, not just the Douglas clan but former exiles in England who had enjoyed his council and friendship, therefore there would be few who would challenge his return.

James would have a private interview with Archibald, where the latter's part in the murder were discussed. The details of the discussion are not recorded although it seems that Archibald succeeded in explaining how complex and dangerous the political environment was at the time of the murder. It is possible knowing the character of Archibald that he may have pointed a finger at Mary's role in the murder, seeking to further alienate James from his mother. James would later make a statement addressed to Archibald; 'I myself, do believe you are innocent of my father's murder, except in foreknowledge and concealing: a fault so common in those days, that no man of any dealing could misknow (be ignorant of), and yet so perilous to be revealed, in respect of all the actors of that tragedy, that no man, without extreme danger, could utter any speech thereof, because they did see it and could not amend it.' James had offered this defence on behalf of Archibald, the same defence which had failed James Douglas, Earl of Morton and sent him to execution. A trial would be arranged in which Archibald was charged with being 'art and part' in the murder. Of the nineteen jurors only nine showed, substitutes were found amongst the friends and factions of the Douglass. There was no witnesses called to accuse Archibald, and depositions of convicted and executed accomplices of Bothwell were offered although they did not mention Archibald. The testimony of his servant John Binning was challenged, he had said they were both present and that Archibald had lost a velvet mule or slipper which was claimed was used to muffle the sound of his footsteps. There was a slipper discovered at the scene which had been identified as Archibald's, and when examined at the trial he would argue that it would be too difficult to walk over the ground from his house in Edinburgh to the scene whilst wearing a slipper over armour. Archibald would be acquitted of the charges during the mockery of a trial. He would be reinstated in his estates and rank, and would later be appointed ambassador to England.

The Babington Plot

The Anglo-Scot League of July 31st, 1586, agreed by Scotland and England, effectively killed off Mary's hopes of liberation and restoration through 'The Association' with her son. Mary would believe that her fate was indefinite captivity, with death offering the only means of escape. The conspiracies to free her by armed force and violence had failed, the recent endeavours by Throckmorton and Parry, the former plotting to pave the way for Spanish invasion, the latter planning the assassination of Elizabeth, had forced Mary to be more cautious in her communications. Nevertheless her supporters were still active. John Savage a English Catholic officer who had served with the Duke of Parma in the Spanish army became involved with some priests at Rheims. They convinced him that murdering the excommunicated Elizabeth would be an act that would be sanctioned by God. He decided to be the instrument to deliver death to the Queen of Elizabeth, and methods were discussed; whether a knife, or shooting her when she was at chapel, or when she walked in her gardens. Mary's agent Thomas Morgan and her exiled supporter Charles Paget would consult with Savage, and the latter with their help would travel to England for the purpose of carrying out his scheme. A priest called John Ballard would also be brought into the conspiracy, and during Lent Ballard would meet with Morgan, Paget and the Spanish ambassador Mendoza in Paris. Learning of Savage's mission in England, Ballard rushed to London to arrange a plan to liberate Mary after Elizabeth was killed. He also hoped that these events would be followed by a Spanish invasion.

Upon arriving in London John Ballard disguised himself as a soldier with the name Captain Fortescue, and was accompanied by a man called Maud who would act as a messenger between London and Paris. Maud would later be revealed as an English agent. Ballard would meet with Anthony Babington, a young Catholic gentleman of good family from Derbyshire who was committed to the cause of Mary.

For the past two years Babington's role as page to Mary's jailer the Earl of Shrewsbury had assisted him in becoming a vital link in the lines of communication between Mary and the Archbishop of Glasgow, Morgan and Paget. He would travel between England and France delivering secret correspondence to and fro. After Mary was transferred from the Earl of Shrewsbury to Paulet it was near impossible for him to pass correspondence from one to the other. John Ballard would offer him some fresh hope. Babington offered a list of possible safe places for Spanish troops to embark, as well as an estimated number of English who would join. He also had a plan on how to liberate Mary from Chartley where she was guarded by fifty armed men. He was interested in getting involved in the assassination plan, offering to help the prospective assassin John Savage by proposing five trusted friends as support, if one failed then another would take his place. These individuals were named as Abington, Barnwell, Charnock, Tilney and Titchbourne. After the meeting with Ballard, Babington would arrange gatherings with friends at St Giles, and elsewhere in London. The invasion would be discussed although the assassination plan was not; this remained confined to only a few individuals.

Mary's secret communication network had however been infiltrated. Her agent in France Thomas Morgan had been imprisoned in the Paris Bastille by the French king Henry III at the insistence of Elizabeth after the full discovery of the Throckmorton plot. Henry refused to extradite Morgan and the latter continued, despite being behind French prison walls, to keep up his intrigues and correspondence on behalf of Mary. On January 1586 he passed a letter to Mary through a new messenger Gilbert Gifford, a seminary priest from a family on Staffordshire. His family had been persecuted by the Protestants and his father was in the Tower of London. He would portray such zeal for the counter-reformation and for Mary's cause that he won the confidence of Morgan. Gifford though was an agent for Francis Walsingham and each step he took he kept the spymaster informed. A new mode of smuggling correspondence out of Chartley Castle was to be employed, where it was collected by a brewer who visited the castle weekly to deliver beer, and brought out in an empty beer barrel. The brewer would then pass the letters to a sympathetic family near Chartley who would then pass then on to a family near London. They would then pass them to the French ambassador M. de Chateauneuf in London. He would need to decipher the letters which would obviously be coded, and Gilbert Gifford had visited Chateauneuf on March 1st 1586 with a letter of introduction from Mary and a new cipher to read the letters. The French ambassador was unhappy about this new mode of communication which had its risks, yet he would be persuaded to hand Gifford a collection of letters which had been stored in the embassy for the purpose of passing on to Mary. With Gifford now having access to letters to and from the French embassy, as well as the cipher, Walsingham was now more aware of the extent of Mary's network of supporters and their schemes. He would employ two agents to handle the intercepted correspondence; Thomas Philips a renowned code-breaker and forger, who would be work with Paulet at Chartley, and one called Gregory, an expert in breaking open letters and resealing them as if untouched. To avoid discover Walsingham would allow the original letters to reach their destinations whilst his agents made copies of the incriminating evidence and deciphered them using the ciphers and codebooks provided by Gilbert Clifford.

During the spring of 1586 Mary would receive a letter dated May 9th 1586 from Thomas Morgan who suggesting that she restores communication with Anthony Babington. This was done through Gilbert Clifford allowing Walsingham to discover the full extent of the plot against Elizabeth and how far Mary had entered into it. According to copies of letters presented at Mary's trial later in the year, Babington would write revealing the plans for a Spanish invasion; for her liberty; and what was to be the fate of Queen Elizabeth where he declares: 'As regards getting rid of the usurper, from subjection to whom we are absolved by the act of excommunication issued against her, there are six gentlemen of quality, all of them my intimate friends, who, for the love they bear to the Catholic cause and to your majesty's service will undertake the tragic execution. It remains now that, according to your infinite desert and your majesty's goodness, their heroic enterprise should be honestly recompensed in themselves if they escape with their lives, or I their posterity if they fall, and that I may give them this assurance by your majesty's authority.' Mary would reply that plans for a Spanish invasion and English rising should be made ready: 'Affairs being thus prepared, then shall it be time to set the gentlemen to work; taking order, upon the accomplishing of their design, I may suddenly be transported out of the place, and that all your forces in the same time be on the field to meet me whilst we wait the arrival of help from abroad, which must be hastened with diligence.' She also offered three means of effecting her escape, one being that whilst she out riding with a usual escort of 18 to 20 horse, that around fifty men on horseback ambush the party and free her. A second idea was for the barns and stables to be set on fire at midnight and whilst the castle guard and servants are diverted a company of men are employed to free her. A third involved blocking the gates when they opened to allow in carts of supplies for the castle. This would be done by lodging specially prepared carts under the raised gates, and then a force of men would enter the castle.

In a packet of letters smuggled out of Chartley Castle on May 20th, one letter sent to Bernardino de Mendoza, the Spanish ambassador in Paris, made a astonishing proposal that in the case that she die and James her son remains a Protestant then she was willing to name Philip of Spain as her successor to the crown of England, and asked in return for this proposal that Spain place her under his protection. She asked that such a proposal be kept secret as she did not want to stoke the jealousy of France. In a letter to her Paris agent Charles Paget, she sought to learn whether Philip intended attacking England to revenge himself against Leicester's actions in the Netherlands and Francis Drake's pirate acts in the West Indies. If there was to be a Spanish expedition she would endeavour to seek the support or neutrality of her son, and if that is not achieved she would seek to form a band of supporters in Scotland, with Lord Claude Hamilton as leader. In the event of James being put in the custody of Lord Claude, and if he does not support the Spanish enterprise then Lord Claude is to hand James over to the Pope or Philip. Lord Claude would also be made Regent of Scotland, with the aim of supporting Spain or at least preventing any Scots from supporting Elizabeth.

Letters such as above and more were copied by Walsingham's agents and by the summer he decided it was time to act. He approached Elizabeth with details of the invasion and assassination plot. Horrified she demanded that the conspirators be arrested, Walsingham however sought to act with some subtlety. One of his agents Maud, a confidant of Ballard, was ordered to denounce Ballard as a Jesuit. With this charge made against Ballard, Babington fearing discovery would briefly flee London, then returned to brave it out even visiting Walsingham who gave no indication that he considered him a traitor. Babington would return to his lodgings, and on the following day August 4th he would learn that Ballard had been captured. With the danger that Ballard under torture would reveal the full extent of the conspiracy Babington and his associate Savage decided to carry on with the assassination plan and gathered their fellow conspirators. However Babington believed he was being followed by Walsingham's agents, and they fled to St Johns Wood. The English Council issued a proclamation with the names of the conspirators and called for their arrest. Babington and his friends were apprehended near Harrow and brought to the Tower of London. They were tortured and full confessions were made pointing the finger at Mary's involvement in a plot to murder Elizabeth.

Mary would be unaware of this doings when she was invited to go out hunting by Paulet on August 8th. She took along her secretaries Nau and Curle, and some servants. It was on the road that the party was met by Sir Thomas George who informed Mary that Babington had been arrested and that she was to be taken to Tixall Castle. First she was bitterly disappointed that this latest attempt at freedom had been undone, and then she recovered her bearings and called on her servants to defend her. Nau and Curle, and her servants were overcome, and Mary was escorted to Tixall by Paulet and his guards. This allowed one of the Privy Council, Mr Waad who arrived at Chartley, and entering Mary's apartment he and his helpers gathered all of Mary's papers and documents and took them to London. Mary would remain under close confinement at Tixall until August 23rd when she was escorted by Paulet and 140 mounted gentlemen of the district.

Mary's secretaries Nau and Curle were placed at Walsingham's house under his custody. Up to the beginning of September they were constantly examined, and whilst they admitted there was correspondence between Babington and Mary they initially refused to reveal any knowledge that would implicate Mary in an assassination plot. There was enough evidence, through correspondence with Scotland, France, Spain and the English Catholics to accuse her of compliance in a plot to escape her custody and support a Spanish invasion, yet Walsingham wanted to score the charge of High Treason levelled against her. The interrogators now threatened Nau and Curle with the rack, they needing to know how the letters to Babington were composed. Nau explained that usually Mary dictated and Nau took notes. The letter to Babington was different as it was presented to Nau in the form of rough notes in Mary's handwriting. Curle translated and put the form into cipher which was then sent off. Nau was also compelled to write a letter to Elizabeth in which he admitted that Mary was part of the conspiracy but made the excuse that she was manipulated into taking part.

On September 13th Babington and thirteen fellow conspirators were put on trial, and all the evidence against them, letters, correspondence and confessions was presented. They were found guilty on September 17th, and on September 20th Babington, Ballard, Savage, Barnwell, Titchbourne, Dunn and Charnock endured the full rigours of the law by the special command of Elizabeth. The following day, possibly sensitive to the public shock of the punishments, the other seven conspirators were executed in the usual fashion. On the afternoon of September 21st Nau and Curle were once more interrogated this time by Lord Burghley, the chancellor Bromley and Sir Christopher Hatton, and knowing the full horror of the fate that awaited them they confessed that the letter to Babington was a genuine reflection of Mary's rough notes, and that she was complicit in the plan to employ six gentlemen assassins. Curle also admitted he burned the original rough notes at Mary's instructions.

The evidence and confessions won from Nau and Curle was enough in the opinion of the Privy Council to corroborate the confessions of Babington and his friends. It was decided they had enough to proceed with a trial using the 27th statute where a capital offence would be laid against anyone claiming the crown of England or attempting to seize it through foreign invasion or assassination. Mary was moved from Chartley to Fotheringay on September 25th. A high court of justice was commissioned by Elizabeth on October 5th to consist of forty-six jury members made up of peers, councillors, judges and lawyers. On October 6th Mary was presented by Paulet with a letter from Elizabeth where she wrote that she was to be tried for conspiring against her life and state. Mary would reply that as a royal queen she would not subjugate herself to such a trial. She also declined on the grounds that she had no one to give her council, she was ignorant of the laws and statutes of the land, she had no knowledge to the standing of the peers that would be judging her, and she had no access to her papers.

Sir Christopher Hatton would visit her and in a private interview inform Mary that by not answering the charges against her many would consider a refusal as an indication of guilt. He also handed a letter from Elizabeth which complained to Mary that: 'You have in various ways attempted to deprive me of my life, and to bring ruin on my kingdom by shedding of blood. I have never proceeded so hardly against you; but, on the contrary, have cherished, and preserved you as faithfully as if you were my own self. Your treasons will be proved and made manifest to you in the place you now are. For this reason it is my pleasure that you answer to the nobility and barons of my kingdom, as you would do myself if I were in person; and as my last injunction I charge and command you to reply to them. I have heard of your arrogance; but act candidly, and you may meet with more favour.' Mary faced with this letter and possibly given hope by the last line of Elizabeth's offering 'favour' if she acted 'candidly' she consented to appear at the trial. The commissioners scheduled the trial to be held at Fotheringay for October 14th.

The Trial of Mary

With the discovery of Mary's part in the Babington Plot, the Earl of Leicester had, according to Spottiswood, been prepared to support having Mary poisoned. The English secretary Francis Walsingham disagreed, saying such a course would harm the reputation of Elizabeth, even if the cause of death was unproven. He wanted a trial, and for Mary to be examined under the law of England. He would write to James informing him of the plot against Elizabeth. Walsingham would also contact Patrick, Master of Gray to sound out James's attitude towards a trial, and for him to suggest there would be bad grace if James sought to mediate for a mother who had been hard on his father. James would instruct Gray to write to Walsingham, to congratulate Elizabeth in uncovering the plot, but also to inform the English secretary that 'it cannot stand well his honour that he be a consenter to take his mother's life, but he is content how strictly she be kept, and all her old knavish servants hanged.'

In writing to James, Walsingham also provided details of the Babington Plot and the accusations and evidence against Mary, even providing extracts of the correspondence between Mary and Babington. He also sent copies of letters which Mary had written to her agent Charles Paget in Paris, in which Mary planned to have Claude Hamilton seize James in a coup, with the possibility of sending him to Spain or the pope. Walsingham sought to show Mary's attitude towards her son was indifferent to the act of depriving him of the crown and using him as a pawn in a political game. She had been prepared to offer John Hamilton,

Lord Arbroath the place of heir apparent if her son should die childless.

The Master of Gray wrote to Archibald on October 11th with his opinion of Mary's supporters that they 'desired any good to Mary as a staff to their own heads', and as for James he was content for the trial to go ahead and believed 'foreign princes should know her crimes' yet in regards to her punishment James did not believe Elizabeth would allow execution where 'she resaves (receives) favour through her clemency', her reputation being esteemed. Unfortunately James would underestimate the power of feeling in England raging against her mother, such that even Elizabeth would struggle to stem.

On the day of the trial, nine o'clock in the morning, Mary was escorted into the great hall of Fotheringay by her physician Burgoin and Sir Andrew Melville. Fotheringay, which is now demolished, was a large motte and bailey castle. The large motte, or mound on which the castle was built on, was surrounded by a large water-filled moat, with a polygonal stone keep. The bailey was secured through ramparts and a ditch, and inside was a great hall and other buildings. Several hundred men guarded the castle.

The commissioners in the Great Hall were seated on benches on each side in the style of a court of justice. To represent Queen Elizabeth at the upper end was a chair and canopy of state surmounted with the arms of England. Mary wore a dress of black velvet, with a veil of white lawn thrown over her. She walked with difficulty as if suffering from lameness or an injury. In the middle of the hall she bowed to the lords and then learning that they were to place her seat below that of the empty seat of state she protested against this treatment of a queen who had once been married to a king of France, yet acknowledging she would find no one to back her up she spoke out: 'Alas! Here are many counsellors, yet there is not one for me.' She then regained her composure and sat down. After the terms and purpose of the trial were read out she addressed the commissioners, complaining of her treatment by England since crossing the border, and challenging the legality of the proceeding. As she was a queen she considered no one to be her superior except for God alone. With her servants as witnesses she stated that any answers she made during this trial was under protest. William Cecil, Lord Burleigh replied that all persons within England were subject to the law, including Mary.

The proceedings began when the crown sergeant, Gawdy, revealed the extent of the conspiracy and Mary's part in it, and her knowledge and encouragement of invasion plans and assassination plots against Elizabeth. The confessions of the executed Babington and his co-conspirators were produced and laid on a table to be studied by the commissioners, as well as Mary's letters to Babington and others, and the confessions of Nau and Curle. A copy of a long letter from Babington to Mary was shown; although Mary would ask why not show the original? And if it is in cipher why not compare it with the copy? Mary would also insist that she had never met Babington, and that she had not written a response to his long letter. She also denied knowledge of letters attributed to her, and claimed she had no part of an assassination plot against Elizabeth: 'I do not deny, that I have longed for liberty, and earnestly tried to regain it. To this nature impelled me; but I call God to witness that I have never conspired against the life of the Queen of England. I confess I wrote to my friends, soliciting their aid to escape these miserable prisons, in which I, a captive queen, have been confined for nineteen years; but I never wrote the letters now produced against me. I confess also that I have written in favour of the persecuted Catholics; and had I been able, or were I even now able, to free them from their miseries by shedding my own blood, I would have done it. But what connection has this with any plot against the life of the queen? And how can I answer for the dangerous designs of others which are carried on without my knowledge?'

Lord Burleigh would respond to her points and would outline all details of the conspiracy and how the copies were corroborated by confessions and a pack of circumstantial evidence. Mary would challenge the legal proceedings, Babington and his co-conspirators had been executed so speedily which denied her the opportunity to cross examine them. She neither was allowed to cross-examine her secretaries Nau and Curle. She had dictated letters to Nau and Curle which were put into cipher, yet she had no way of investigating whether they added details into the ciphered letters which she had no knowledge of. She also put forward the possibility that they had received letters addressed to her, which they failed to deliver, instead answering and adding details without her knowing, putting these replies into cipher and using her name. She also stated that not being able to study the original of Babington's long letter to her, and to compare it to his confession, she had no way of determining whether the confession was written in Babington's own handwriting. She would labour the points that she had no access to her private papers and notes which had been seized in Chartley, she had no council to support her, and no witnesses were produced of which she could cross-examine.

Mary would ask whether forgeries were being used against her: 'What security have I that these are my very ciphers?' She would address Walsingham; 'a young man lately in France has been detected forging my alphabets (ciphers). Think you, Mr Secretary, that I am ignorant of your devices used so craftily against me?' She would imply strongly that Walsingham may have forged her ciphers, 'how can I be assured that he hath not counterfeited my ciphers to bring me to my death? Walsingham in turn rose and exclaimed: 'I call God to witness that I have done nothing as a private person that is unworthy of an honest man, or, as a public servant, anything unbecoming my office; but I plead guilty to have been exceedingly careful of the safety of the queen and this realm.' He also added that 'if the traitor Ballard had himself offered me his help in the investigation, I would not have refused it.' In other words he would have done what is necessary to protect Queen and country. After Mary's arguments Lord Burleigh and some crown lawyers would once more go through the evidence, then the trial was adjourned until the next day.

The following morning October 15th, Mary would once more proclaim that as a sovereign monarch she was answerable to no one. However, without counsel to support her which she complained of, she decided that she could not deny knowledge of the letters. She would admit sending letters to Morgan and Paget in France, and the Spanish ambassador Mendoza, as well as the notes that she had passed to her secretaries in regard to correspondence with Babington. She would confess that she had conspired for her own escape, but denied that she was part of a plot to kill the Queen of England, claiming that any such written evidence alluding to that had been asserted by others. She would make a long speech regarding her treatment since entering England in search of sanctuary and protection from Elizabeth, which she believed the latter had promised through the token of a ring. With this ring on her finger she displayed it to the commissioners: 'Here it is my lords: look at it well: it came from your royal mistress. Trusting to that pledge of love and protection, I came amongst you and you know how that pledge has been redeemed.' Once more she declared her innocence and 'being a queen, she should be believed upon the word of a queen.' Lord Burghley responded by once more going through the evidence whilst facing many interruptions from Mary who refuted the evidence and the witness testimonies. Mary also sought another day to present her defence before the commissioners, this was seemingly denied, with the trial being broken up due to a secret instruction from Elizabeth to Lord Burghley asking the trial to be adjourned until October 25th and relocated to Westminster. The commissioners were also to present themselves before Elizabeth with a record of the two days of legal proceedings.

Mary was to remain at Fotheringay with Paulet, called the 'Queen of the Castle' by Lord Burghley. The commissioners would gather at the Star Chamber in Westminster and the trial would recommence. Here the record of the trial at Fotheringay was presented, and following that Nau and Curle were examined once again, reconfirming their previous statements. Whilst the evidence was being considered it was proclaimed by the judges that whatever sentence was made against Mary would not affect her son James's claims to the English succession. When a verdict was reached, Mary would be found guilty of being privy to the assassination plot against Elizabeth.

On October 29th a parliament would be summoned to consider the verdict, which would be approved by both the House of Commons and House of Lords. They petitioned Elizabeth to proclaim the verdict publicly, which was granted quickly, leading to reported outpourings of joy by the people. The two Houses also sought the sentence of death for Mary, citing the Bible and the example of God's anger when Saul showed mercy to Agag, and when Ahab gave Benhadad a pardon. They argued that to spare Mary would endanger Elizabeth's life, the security of the Protestant religion and of the nation. Receiving this petition Elizabeth sent a reply on November 12th thanking God for the preservation of her life and for the widespread affection showed by her subjects. Outwardly she was loath to pronounce death against Mary, and on November 14th she sent Sir Christopher Hatton with word to the House of Commons asking whether there was a means to pardon and spare Mary's life, and at the same time ensure the safety and welfare of Elizabeth and England. On November 18th both Houses gave reply that if Mary was placed under closer confinement this would not end the plots against Elizabeth's life, and if Mary was sent out of the kingdom she would return at the head of an armed invasion. They offered a prayer to heaven that Elizabeth, for the sake of religion, the security of the nation, and for the preservation of Elizabeth's life, that the sentence of death against Mary should be executed. Elizabeth gave an answer that was vague and ambiguous: 'If I should say to you that I mean not to grant your petition, by my faith, I should say unto you more than perhaps I mean; and if I should say unto you I mean to grant your petition, I should then tell you more than it is fit for you to know: and so I must deliver you an answer answerless.' With this reply she dismissed the messengers from the Houses, no doubt perplexed.

Mary was informed of the verdict passed by the judges, which was ratified by the Parliament. Despite the ambiguity of Elizabeth, Mary was assured that she would receive no mercy and to help her prepare for execution she was offered a Protestant minister. Mary refused this offer stating that before God she had been chosen to die for the Catholic faith, in which the messengers said she would not be considered a martyr as she had plotted the death of Elizabeth, a charge which she once more denied.

Mary was from that day deprived of all rights of a queen and to be treated as a private person, her jailer Paulet ensured that her arms and regalia were taken away, and even distractions like her billiards table were removed.

The Ambassadors

The French ambassador Chanteauneuf in London, writing to M. d'Esteval on October 20th, considered that there was little practical support for Mary to be found in France. Henry III, king of France, Mary's brother-in-law, would however act for honour's sake and urge the French secretary in Scotland, M. de Courcelles to incite James to more vigorous action in defence of Mary. Courcelles's initial opinion when attending the king at Falkland Palace was that James considered this a matter for Elizabeth, and Mary had only herself to blame. James also believed that Mary's life was not in danger and added that although he 'loved her as much as nature or duty bound him'; she 'bore him as little good will as she did the Queen of England.' There was anger amongst the Scots nobles, such as Angus, Huntley, Lord Claude Hamilton, and Lord Herries at the superiority that Elizabeth claimed over Mary, and the Earl of Bothwell was reported to have said that if James does not act in defence of his mother then he should be hanged. In conversations with George Douglas, James would argue that Mary had conspired to take the crown from his head.

Such pressure from the nobility, as well as growing public anger persuaded James to send Sir William Keith to England as additional ambassador. John Maitland, secretary of state would advise James to threaten to end the Anglo-Scot league if Mary executed, and the Master of Gray would write to Archibald Douglas on October 21st, informing him that Maitland, who was an enemy of Archibald, gave 'plain advice to the king, that if England stand strict at this time, then they are no more to be trusted, and foreigners to be sought.' It was suspected by many that the present ambassador in London, Archibald Douglas, was in the employ of Elizabeth and Walsingham, and it was said that 'as he had been of the father's (Lord Darnley) murder, he would have his hand as deep in the mother's death.' He would use the information provided by the Master of Gray to inform his English friends that Maitland could not be trusted, and ever since the summer Walsingham had been ignoring his letters. There was a belief that Archibald was making assertions that James cared more for his rights to the English succession than he did the life of his mother.

Archibald Douglas would write to James dated October 16th, responding to a letter of September 28th where James had instructed him to intercede for Mary's life, and also to insure his own rights to the English succession. On the first point Archibald had been at court in early October and whilst Elizabeth had assured him that she did not like this 'proceeding against her (Mary) by order of justice', she explained that the 'Association', the body of English subjects who swore a bond to prosecute to the death anyone involved in a assassination plot against Elizabeth, were urging Elizabeth to 'let the law have its course against the Scottish queen, because so long as she continued to plot, the life of Elizabeth and the safety of England would be in constant danger.' It was their arguments that persuaded Elizabeth to proceed with the trial. On the second point regarding James's succession claims to the English throne, Archibald believed that if James was too earnest in wanting Mary's life saved then their would be a suspicion amongst some English ministers that the rumour and reports of a agreement between James and Mary where they share sovereignty was true. Archibald suggested that James make a statement in the Scottish parliament stating that he was innocent of agreeing to a joint rule with his mother

With Elizabeth's knowledge and permission Archibald had been in negotiations with both Protestants and Catholics. Archibald would note that the Protestants were determined to prosecute Mary, and he had to convince Elizabeth that the reason he wanted to meet with Catholics was to inform them of James's 'late behaviour towards her (Mary)' which suggests he was discouraging them of any ideas and notions that James would intervene in a significant manner.

Having decided to send Sir William Keith, who would prove resolute enough in pleading for Mary's life, James would write to Archibald Douglas with strong words: "Admonishes him to be instant in 'earnest dealing' for Queen Mary: if 'her life be lost,' James will have no more traffic with England, and if Douglas values the enjoyment of the royal favour he must 'spare nae pains nor plainness in this case,' but carry out the instructions given to William Keith."

The French king Henry III would send Monsieur de Bellievre to London to intercede on behalf of Mary. He would receive an audience with Elizabeth on November 28th. He would argue that Mary should not be tried and judged as a private individual, she was a sovereign princess who had crossed into England seeking the hospitality of Elizabeth. He also stated that Henry III would show gratitude if Elizabeth showed mercy, whereas Elizabeth replied that through Mary, she, England and the Protestant religion had been the subjects of plots and intrigues. She would have Mary's life saved if such a course was consistent with her safety and that of her kingdom. Bellievre would warn that whilst there were English Catholics who supported Mary, they would transfer this patronage to another more dangerous master if Mary was killed. He suggested Philip of Spain and spoke of the machinations of the Spanish: 'If it is pretended, that your Catholic subjects are less obedient to you on account of the stay of the Queen of Scots, your good sense will enable you to see that there is no good reason to fear such a feeble support; and on this point I will tell you madam, what I have been assured is true by an honourable personage, that a certain minister of a prince whom you have reason to suspect openly declares that it would be a good thing for his master's greatness that the Queen of Scotland were already dead, for he is very certain that the English Catholic party would range itself entirely on his master's side.' Elizabeth would explain that unless there was a solution which allowed her to reign safely whilst allowing Mary to live, then she would grateful if such were forwarded. There was to be another interview scheduled for December 5th, this however would be deferred until January 6th.

Sir William Keith would arrive in London during early November. In conference with Archibald it was decided that the commission should be divided up, with Archibald negotiating for James's rights to the succession whilst Keith negotiated for Mary's life. Both Keith and Archibald Douglas would be invited on November 22nd to a banquet with Lord Burghley, Francis Walsingham, and other members of the Privy Council, and they outlined the whole case that had been made against Mary. They also assured that James's claims to the English succession were not prejudiced, although when asked by the Scots that such commitment should be expressed in written terms they made no commitment except promising to put this to the Queen.

A letter from Archibald Douglas to the Master of Gray, dated November 22nd, suggests there were perhaps two private audiences with Elizabeth, in which Keith 'both sufficiently and well delivered' his embassy to the queen. Elizabeth would argue 'it would be useless to spare Mary's life and trust to her gratitude, because, although she might refrain from plotting, her supporters were confident that she would reward them if they succeeded in setting her on the throne of Elizabeth.' She feared that the English Catholics would continue to conspire to return England to papal authority through the figurehead of Mary. The Earl of Leicester would arrive at court from Flanders on the evening of November 23rd.

A further audience with Elizabeth and some of her 'learned council' would be set for November 29th, and Keith delivered a letter from James in which he hoped that the execution would not be carried through and also expressed how as a son and king it would shame him not to try and stop it. Elizabeth would reply to Keith that she wished no harm to Mary, and would give one of her arms if both she and Mary could live in safety, yet there was ministerial and public pressure placed on her to sign the warrant for execution. Keith asked if the proceedings against Mary could be stayed until James could send further word, this Elizabeth refused as she said that any leniency towards Mary would be looked on unfavourably by her people who clamoured for her life. James had also announced he would send another ambassador to plead the cause of Mary, although Elizabeth doubted this would make a difference

On November 30th Archibald Douglas would receive a letter from the Master of Gray dated November 23rd, where he is informed that through 'common report' James VI believes that Archibald has 'been a ill instrument' in 'matters concerning Mary's safety. Archibald would write to James dated December 8th refuting these allegations, and outlining the meetings and proceedings he has been involved, as well as reporting on the attitude of ministers and the English people.

The Master of Gray also sent several letters to Keith, one of which was also dated November 23rd 'at his Majesty's direction', where he was to declare 'to the Queen and Council of England that his Majesty would consider rigorous proceedings against his mother as an irreparable breach of kindly relations with him.' There was also an insulting statement against Elizabeth's father Henry VIII, whose; 'reputation was never prejudged in anything but in the beheading of his bedfellows.' When Keith delivered these words on December 6th, it 'threw Elizabeth into a towering rage', and according to Archibald Douglas it was the Earl of Leicester who managed 'to appease her.'

The Earl of Leicester would blame the tone of the letter not on the king but on some 'mischief-maker'. Lord Burghley would write on December 6th to both Archibald Douglas and William Keith stating that if not for such a 'strange and unseasonable message, as did directly toward her noble father, herself, and all the estates of her present Parliament, she would not have misliked or denied his Majesty's request.' Lord Burghley considered that the composer of the letter had been seeking to 'stir up trouble, or to tempt her (Elizabeth) to carry out the sentence at once'. Elizabeth would not at that time allow a safe-conduct for an embassy, or delay the execution of Mary, yet would listen to any offers made by Douglas and Keith if they are presented within 10 to 12 days. Francis Walsingham would write to Douglas and Keith on December 7th, they had sent a quick letter to Lord Burghley which was passed to Elizabeth; she in turn would allow James to send for a small embassy to pass into England.

Walsingham would write to John Maitland of Thirlestane, Secretary of State on December 8th, the first time for five months. He would admit that Maitland was widely blamed for the tone of the message delivered by Sir

William Keith, although Walsingham claimed he held 'of another opinion.' He would write that "some here would like to see the rupture of the present amity, which would be more for the advantage of the 'common enemies' than of our sovereigns". He was also express how many in England were surprised that 'their brethren in Scotland earnestly urge the king to plead his mother's cause, seeing that all papists in Europe hope to re-establish their religion in both our realms by means of her.' Whilst Maitland would not win entirely win the confidence of Walsingham, it appears that suspicion regarding the aggressive tone of the message delivered by Keith would pass to the Master of Gray

After James learned of Elizabeth's anger he would backtrack, and intended to dispatch Sir Robert Melville and Patrick, Master of Gray to England to plead for his mother's life. He would write to Elizabeth claiming that she had misunderstood his meaning, and meant to inform her on 'how incensed the country is' about the verdict made by the English parliament against his mother. Walsingham wrote to James suggesting that he prioritise his succession rights to the crown of England rather than for the life of his mother who would deprive him of the crown of Scotland.

The choice of Melville and Gray as ambassadors angered the nobility, as they were considered minor figures. A popular choice was John Maitland of Thirlestane, Secretary of State, yet he was reluctant due to the recent suspicions against him, and to James he was too indispensable in domestic matters to be allowed to go. Francis Stuart, Earl of Bothwell offered his services although he was considered too much of a Mary loyalist to be trusted on such an important embassy. The nobility though were stirring; Huntley, Crawford, Montrose, Athol, and ominously the

Earl of Arran were talking up the possibility of war. A convention was called in November for the purpose of raising a tax in the event of war if Mary is executed, with the nobility offering a voluntary contribution. The burghs though refused, the economic benefits of peace with England outweighed the financial chaos of conflict.

Archibald Douglas would also write a letter to James in early December in the name of the Earl of Leicester, who was equally angry at the tone of the recent correspondence. He would write that it was rumoured that James sought to save Mary's life because he had entered into a secret agreement in which he would place her claim to the English succession before his, and had also entered into talks with foreign powers. It was clear that Archibald was close to the Earl of Leicester, and Keith would complain that whilst Archibald would claim that Leicester 'thought that Mary must die', he had not been able to speak with him alone to learn Leicester's true opinion. It would however be clear that Leicester in later letters to James considered that the king should deal 'more moderately' for the life of Mary, and he would remind him that 'Mary's will would dispossess you, both of the crown of Scotland and of your claim to that of England.' He would also point out that Elizabeth's death 'might be as prejudicial to your interests, as your mother's liberty would formerly have been.' Leicester was clearly attempting to convince James to consider the practicalities and advantages in the death of his mother, and Archibald Douglas was a trusted associate of his. Leicester also assigned Thomas Randolph, 'a guid instrument' according to Archibald to assist combating these rumours spoke against James in regards to an *Association* with his mother.

It was about this time that Keith began to suspect Archibald Douglas of chicanery. In a letter to Maitland, dated December 9th he would term Archibald 'the personage' who 'is in a difficult position and knows not where to turn.' Archibald had received word from the Master of Gray that he should not return to Scotland due to the widespread belief he was deliberately undermining the mission to save Mary's life. Keith's letter implies that Archibald being fearful of returning to Scotland was now working to ensure his survival in England, of which Keith would respond that the King of Scots is young and Elizabeth was 'ane auld queen', and if James succeeds to the throne of England Archibald would also 'lose England' as a refuge. Archibald would state that he 'would do his best for the king, so long as he spared his life', but Keith would consider that Archibald was a 'serpent in a man's likeness' and 'does not care a whit for this matter'.

Keith would also in the same letter to Maitland write that the English blamed the Master of Gray for the 'hard letter' which James sent to the Queen of England, and the Earl of Leicester now 'speaks no guid of him'. It was suspected that the Master of Gray was of the French interest, and it appears that the French King Henry III began to support a more assertive line in defence of Mary, for honour's sake seeking to appear as if doing all possible to save Mary, yet Archibald Douglas would report in a letter to the Master of Gray dated December 15th that the French ambassador in London was spreading a rumour that the Scots embassy would bring to England a declaration of war, which was one of the reasons that the English were delaying passports. If this is true then the French motives are difficult to fathom; possibly they were hoping to cause a breach between Scotland and England in regards to the recent Anglo-Scot League; or perhaps they were using such tactics to genuinely pressure

Elizabeth to mitigate her intentions against Mary. However, Archibald Douglas would in the New Year be accused of spreading rumours about the French ambassadors that they were conspiring against Elizabeth, so perhaps his report was part of an effort to sow suspicions in Scotland and undermine French influence. In regard to the new embassy from Scotland, Archibald would inform the Master of Gray that he should not come: 'You coming here can serve no good purpose until you are in greater favour, and have cleared yourself of suspicion.' The Master of Gray would also learn he had an enemy in Francis Walsingham who would ensure his 'credit diminish by lies.' Being close to Leicester and Walsingham, Archibald Douglas would be suspected of acting entirely in the English interest, seeking to undermine the Scottish efforts to save Mary.

The Scottish Parliament sitting in Edinburgh would pass an act of December 15th authorising the sending of ambassadors to foreign rulers in order to complain against the treatment of Mary by Elizabeth. They would be sent to Denmark, France and Spain. Many of Mary's old supporters were at the court of James, such as Huntley and the Hamiltons, and the borderers were getting ready to launch attacks into England. Having appointed Sir Robert Melville and the Master of Gray as ambassadors to plead for Mary's life, he also George Young, clerk of the Privy Council, Sir Alexander Stuart and other assistants and servants to the diplomatic train. Their instructions from the king given on December 17th were for the ambassadors to offer sureties for Mary's life, and that foreign princes will put their names to any pledges or bonds produced. They were to suggest that if Elizabeth fears for her own life she could banish Mary, or imprison her more stringently with 'cautions and obligations' of good behaviour offered by foreign princes. If none of this was acceptable Elizabeth was to suggest what security she would expect in return for sparing Mary's life.

Sir Robert Melville was the second son of Sir John Melville of Raith, and his younger brother was Sir James Melville of Halhill, the famous diplomat who wrote a important autobiography of his life and times which covered his service as a statesman with Mary, Queen of Scots and James VI, and gave character sketches of the likes of Lord Darnley, the Earl of Bothwell, the Earl of Moray, Queen Elizabeth of England and others. Sir Robert was also a career diplomat. Born in 1527/28 he was university schooled and entered early service with Mary of Guise. He would join the Lords of Congregation during the Reformation; his early diplomatic missions winning support from Queen Elizabeth for the Protestant cause, and unsuccessfully lobbying for a marriage between Elizabeth and the Earl of Arran. Melville opposed the marriage of Mary to Lord Darnley and joined the Earl of Moray during his rebellion. After winning a pardon from Mary he became resident ambassador at the English court, but after the murder of Darnley and Mary's marriage to Bothwell, he began to work for the Lords who were in opposition to this new regime in Scotland. When Mary was a captive in Lochleven Castle, he would visit in an unofficial capacity to try to convince her to renounce Bothwell. When she escaped and raised an army for Langside he was by her side, although he was acting as a non-combatant trying to find the means to bring reconciliation. When captured after Langside he was spared and reemployed by the victorious Earl of Moray as a diplomatic envoy to Elizabeth. Melville would develop a loyalty towards Mary, and when she was confined in England he used efforts to try and bring peace and accord between the opposing sides in Scotland. When Kirkcaldy of Grange took command of Edinburgh Castle, Melville joined him. After the fall of Edinburgh Castle on April 1573 he was due to be executed by the Earl of Morton, Regent of Scotland, having been deemed a traitor. He was spared by the intercession of Elizabeth. After a year of incarceration he was released and retired from politics during the remainder of Morton's regency. He would return to court during the ascendancy of Esme Stuart in 1580 and was knighted on October 20th 1581. He would be appointed treasurer-depute to William Ruthven, Earl of Gowrie in August 1581, and whilst taking no part in the Ruthven Raid, he would later help James to escape his captors. He would be appointed a privy councillor in 1583.

Sir Robert Melville would reach Berwick by December 19th where the Master of Gray carried on to Alnwick. Gray would receive correspondence from a secret source in London and send them on to Maitland, adding his own letter describing Archibald as a 'knavery of a man' and warning that Walsingham was 'urging severity in dealing with Queen Mary.' Walsingham had also been briefing against Gray. He travelled further on towards London. Melville and his party would meet with the Master of Gray at Ware on December 30th, who was joined by Archibald Douglas and William Keith. Already there were sharp suspicions about Archibald with Maitland apparently having warned them to be careful with certain information. The four had a consultation at Ware and Archibald was informed that he was suspected in Scotland of undermining attempts to save Mary's life, although it was also added that King James refused to believe the unfavourable reports, that 'a man who has received such great favour would fail to do his duty.' Archibald would for a time convince the others that the reports against him were wrong, although they would wait to see 'if his actions correspond to his words.' The following day they would arrive in London and ask an audience of the Queen of England.

The French ambassador Bellievre would meet with Elizabeth on December 29th and would remain in London for six more days. Elizabeth would send word to the Scots ambassadors that she understood they were accredited with the French ambassador and had already had some communications with Bellievre although they denied this, explaining that they are avoiding meetings with other parties until they had an audience with Elizabeth. The English were wary of any co-ordination of diplomatic efforts by the Scots and French, and Archibald Douglas would be later suspected of informing the English of the instructions of the Scots ambassadors. They would finally meet Elizabeth in the Presence Chamber at Greenwich on January 6th, where according to Melville 'no serious conversations' occurred because of the Christmas festivities. The Queen said that she felt her life would not be safe while Mary lived. Speaking to the Queen, and later with the Earl of Leicester on January 6th, the Scots did not believe there was hope for Mary, and George Young perceived that they 'deal for a dead lady.'

On January 6th the same day as the initial Scottish audience with Elizabeth, the French ambassador Bellievre would have another meeting, his diplomacy this time was harder. He stated that: 'If your Majesty will set at nought such high considerations and disregard the prayers of the king, my master, he has charged me to tell you madam, that he will recant this proceeding as a thing opposed to the common interest of kings, and most especially offensive to himself.' This exchange angered Elizabeth:

'Monsieur de Bellievre, are you commissioned by the King, my brother, to hold this language to me?' Bellievre replied that he was 'expressly commanded by him so to do.' Elizabeth would ask for this authority to be shown to her, expecting it written by the King of France's hand. Bellievre would present the signed commission the following day, and in the Presence Chamber, which Elizabeth had cleared of all except Bellievre, Chateauneuf, and one of her courtiers, they had a private conference for an hour. The French would fail in their negotiations and Elizabeth would command Bellievre to leave England within a few days. She would also send a strong letter to Henry III in which she warned: 'The threat of an enemy will never make me fear; on the contrary it is the surest way to despatch the cause of so many misfortunes. I will never live to see the hour when any prince whatsoever may boast of having humbled me so far that I should drink such a draught of my own dishonour.' The message would cause Henry to cease any aggressive intentions in defence of Mary

George Young would write to Maitland on January 10th, and part of his mission to England seems to have been to deliver correspondence and secret instructions to Walsingham. Whilst Young's intention was to wait before approaching Walsingham, until the result of the initial negotiations, the correspondence may have been a threat to exit the Anglo-Scot League if Mary's life is not spared. The resourceful Archibald Douglas would discover that there was correspondence to be delivered to Walsingham, and fearing that 'this would turn to his prejudice' considering the work he had done in undermining Maitland, he asked Young to reveal the details of this correspondence. Young would avoid this, and he would also write that Douglas had been spreading lies about him in order to undermine any diplomatic credit he might have. He would inform Maitland of the hopelessness of the task in hand. He suspected strongly that Archibald Douglas was not prepared to follow the instructions that James had given Gray and Melville, and Douglas had told Gray that as had not been assured that he could return safely to Scotland he was in no way prepared to offend Elizabeth. Archibald would try to bring Gray to the same opinion. George Young was also fearful of sending letters because of possible interception by the English, and he would relate how letters from Chateauneuf meant for Bellievre was taken forcefully from the two messengers employed in this task. Chateauneuf intended to go to the English court and protest this treatment, and then he would learn that he was to be charged with being 'art and part' in a new conspiracy against Elizabeth.

According to Young, Chateauneuf believed that Archibald Douglas had accused him to the English council. When on January 9th the Scottish ambassadors went to visit Chateauneuf, Archibald made himself scarce with the excuse he was to meet with the Earl of Leicester and also to visit the English court to order horses for King James, an excuse that conveniently allowed him to avoid answering any accusation the French ambassador might make against him. This conspiracy, which the French believed was concocted by Archibald Douglas, would help support those within the English council and parliament set upon executing Mary. The Master of Gray was also of the opinion that this alleged conspiracy had also persuaded Elizabeth to more closely consider the more extreme options.

When the Scots had another meeting with Elizabeth and the Privy Council on January 10th, Sir Robert Melville was vigorous in following his commission, whereas the Council directed 'hard speeches' against him. The Spanish ambassador would learn that Elizabeth accused Melville of encouraging James to take offence at the way his mother was treated, and warning that 'if she had a councillor who gave her such advice as he gave the King of Scotland, she would have his head off, to which he replied that if he were her councillor he would rather lose his head than fail to give her such advice.' All their offers as written in the instructions from the king were refused, and Melville observed 'nothing but extremity towards Mary,' and he believed their 'resolution is already taken.' The Master of Gray would propose that if Mary renounced her claim to the throne of England in place of James this would discourage Catholics from plotting in her interest. The Earl of Leicester stated that this would just replace Mary with James in these conspiracies and Elizabeth exclaimed: 'How is this possible? According to the declaration of law she can convey nothing.' The Master of Gray would reply: 'If she has no rights, you have no cause to fear her; if she has, let her then assign them to her son, who will then have full title to succeed you.' This caused Elizabeth to fly into a fury, 'By God's passion!, that were to cut mine throat; and for a dukedom or an earldom to yourself, you or such as you, would cause some of your desperate knaves to kill me. No, by God!, your master shall never be in that place.' Failing to win Elizabeth's acknowledgment of James's claim to the English throne, and receiving several cutting remarks against his character, the Master of Gray returned to the object of the embassy and asked that Mary's life could be spared for fifteen days so that they could send word to James, of which Elizabeth refused. Melville asked Elizabeth for eight days respite, receiving an abrupt reply, 'No, not for an hour!' Elizabeth then left the chamber.

The Master of Gray would write a report to King James on January 12th, and would also note that after the last audience with Elizabeth, both she and Leicester sought a private audience with him. He would state that he would be 'determined to refuse, so that none should suspect he was 'tied to England.' He also wrote that the Scots ambassadors now intended to seek another audience and to deal as 'sharply' as the French ambassador had done. The Master of Gray would also write to Maitland suggesting he convince James that 'his best way does not lie with friendship with England.' He would call Archibald a 'poison in these negotiations, for his opinion carries much weight.' There were also a great deal of suspicion in regards to the English, with the Scots ambassadors wary of sending their full report as they feared any messengers would be seized. They would present their report once they returned to Scotland, expecting to arrive there on January 24th. The Master of Gray's opinion had hardened against the English and may well be suggestive that he was of the French interest as suspected, with an agenda to exploit the negotiations over Mary, and create splits between Scotland and England, which would inevitably bring advantage to France.

The Scots ambassadors would have another audience with Elizabeth on January 15th, and whilst the Queen according to Sir Robert Melville 'appeared reasonable' the Privy Council 'remained obdurate.' Events would further hamper the ambassador's efforts when Melville would report that letters had arrived from Scotland suggesting that James VI 'takes not this matter to heart'. This appears to be a reference to a pleading letter James sent to Leicester dated December 15th, in which he wrote; "How infatuated and inconsistent I should be 'if I should prefer my mother to the title let all men judge.' My religion ever caused me to hate her policy, although honour compels me to plead for her life." These words could be interpreted to as an admission that the mission of the Scots embassy to save Mary's life was pretence, and the meaning could encourage the English councillors 'to push things to extremity'. George Young on January 20th would write to Maitland stating that through these letters and reports Elizabeth and Leicester were persuaded that in regards to Mary, James 'does all this perfunctionorie and that he could with time digest the worse.' This belief was according to Courcelles, the French secretary in Scotland, also being promoted by Sir Alexander Stuart who claimed he knew the secret mind of James, and would inform Elizabeth and Leicester that the prior embassies to England had been for the show of 'honour and reputation' and that James could be appeased in the event of Mary's execution through gifts of dogs and deer. Stuart was the 2nd son of Alexander Stuart of Scotstounhill, the former captain of Blackness Castle, and a friend of Archibald Douglas.

Alexander Stuart would be approached by Elizabeth and Leicester to transport letters to James VI, despite being prohibited by the Scots ambassadors to do so. Sir Robert Melville considered that Alexander Stuart was not a 'suitable agent', and his intentions to travel to Scotland without the ambassador's consent, and at the biding of Elizabeth and Leicester would 'do harm'. Melville would try to convince Stuart to give up his intentions, yet despite initially agreeing to this request Stuart still intended to go, bragging he 'knows further of his highnesses (James) mind in all their matters.'

The Master of Gray would confirm Melville's report to James VI that the letters from Scotland had damaged their mission, and he asked James to disown Sir Alexander Stuart once he arrives in Scotland. Elizabeth wanted confirmation that James did not care that his mother dies, and it was suspected that Stuart would bring secret assurances to James that he would be confirmed as claimant to the English throne, although not in public. Elizabeth intended keeping the Scots ambassadors in England until Sir Alexander Stuart completed his mission to Scotland, and if he failed then Randolph and Killigrew were to be sent north to 'seele' or hoodwink James away from thoughts of revenge if Mary is executed. Both Gray and Melville would write and ask James not to admit the English ambassadors until he had read their reports.

Gray would be confident that they could secure Mary's life for a few months, even if not gaining a 'full grant' for her safety. He also mentioned that they had made a complaint about dramatic performances being played out for the amusement of the public, where James's mother was brought to the Queen of England with a rope. Whether Gray was a French agent at that time is unclear, he would be successfully prosecuted on the charge of treasonous communication with France several months later; nevertheless Melville would praise his efforts in trying to save Mary, along with that of William Keith and George Young. The Master of Gray has often been said to have been intriguing with Archibald Douglas to ensure the execution of Mary, and whilst they had worked together before, on this occasion this there is little evidence to say they were colluding. If anything Gray was working to save the life of Mary, in direct contrast to the previous summer when he would be accused of writing to Elizabeth, suggesting she should secretly despatch Mary.

As for Sir Alexander Stuart he said to be Archibald Douglas's friend. The latter could not return to Scotland with the letters from Elizabeth and Leicester, but Stuart could, and intended to do so against the orders of the Scots ambassadors.

James would send a letter to Elizabeth dated January 26, a long and passionate plead for the life of his mother, although he would not deliver a strong enough message to cause a breach with England. He would ask her to take the views of his embassy and not those who 'vaunt themselves to know further of my mind in this matter than my ambassadors, I pray you not to think me a chameleon, but by the contrary, them to be malicious impostors, as surely they are.' He would be speaking of Archibald Douglas and Sir Alexander Stuart, both of which had been complained against by Keith, Melville, Gray and Young.

The Scots ambassadors who were expecting to leave for Scotland by January 22nd, would be detained for several days on account of a accusation of being involved in yet another plot against Elizabeth, on account of the Master of Gray sending one of his followers to a friend with a brace of pistols. They would be held back long enough for Sir Alexander Stuart to travel alone to Scotland. James was publicly angered with the behaviour of Sir Alexander Stuart, and as reported by Courcelles he promised to 'hang him before he put his boots off', and 'if the Queen (Elizabeth) meddled with his mother's life, she should know, he would follow somewhat else than dogs or deer.' Once Stuart presented himself to James and delivered the messages from Elizabeth, there was no punishment. Although there are no details of the message or letter it is believed that James was secretly assured of his claim to the English succession.

The Scots ambassadors would be cleared of any conspiracy; there are no details of any proceedings. The Master of Gray would write to Maitland on January 29th reporting of rumours that the Spanish were about to attack or the French under the Duke of Guise had landed in Sussex. There was a report that Fotheringay had been attacked with the intention of freeing Mary, as well as a resurrection in the northern counties in her name. These rumours and reports would raise further cries from the public to have Mary put to death.

The ambassadors would arrive in Scotland on February 7th, Melville would be commended for the energy he had exhibited on behalf of Mary, and later receive from James the gift of a wardship of £1,000 Scots. Sir William Keith would also be rewarded with a grant of estates in Delny. He would be retained as an ambassador, with future missions to Denmark, France and the Netherlands. Peter Young would continue as clerk to the Privy Council. Alexander Stuart's fate is less known although he appears to have continued as a diplomatic envoy.

The Execution

As the Scots ambassadors made their way north, Elizabeth was haunted by the demands that were set upon her; from both her ministers and the public to execute Mary, the former Queen of Scots. This was a heavy burden, and as she neglected amusements for gloomy contemplation she would be heard muttering a Latin, 'Aut fer aut feri; ne feriari feri' (Either bear with her or strike; lest you be struck, strike). Elizabeth dreaded the black reputation she would gain for personally ordering Mary's execution, yet she also understood the many potential dangers that would swirl around her if Mary was allowed to live. Finally on February 1st she sent word for her secretary Davison to bring her the warrant for Mary's execution written up by Lord Burghley. She put her signature to it and asked Davison to take it to the Lord Chancellor to be sealed, and added a comment of black humour when she suggested he could show the warrant to Walsingham, 'but I fear the shock might kill him outright.'

Elizabeth was somewhat vague about when the execution should be followed through, ordering that it should not be held in the open instead in the hall of Fotheringay Castle. It has been suggested that she intended using the order only when an enemy landed on English soil although this is countered when she recalled Davison as he was leaving with the warrant. She then complained of the burden on her shoulders at having ordered such a thing, and queried why Sir Amias Paulet and his colleagues could not have done their duty and relieved her of the burden, the meaning of which Davison interpreted as a wish to secretly kill Mary. Davison would leave Elizabeth and consult with Walsingham, and both drafted a joint letter to Paulet with the suggestion he kill Mary, using the bond of Association as justification. Paulet would refuse this commission, and wrote a strong, angry letter to Walsingham. When Davison was made aware of Paulet's refusal he informed Elizabeth who in a fit of indignant anger cried them 'dainty nice, precise fellows', and accused them of throwing all responsibility onto her whilst promising much through bonds as the 'association' yet performing nothing.

The warrant signed by Elizabeth would be sealed and delivered by Davison to the Privy Council on February 3rd. They would draw up a letter to be sent to the Earl of Shrewsbury, ordering him along with the Earl of Kent and Paulet to proceed with the sentence of execution against Mary.

On February 7th the Earl of Shrewsbury, the Earl of Kent, and Beal, the clerk of the Privy Council arrived at Fotheringay and handed Paulet the warrant for Mary's execution. At two in the afternoon they demanded an audience with Mary in her apartment, this was refused with Mary informing she was indisposed and in bed. Once they insisted that their visit was of utmost importance she gave them admittance, she sitting on her bed with a small table at her feet. The Earl of Shrewsbury told her the reason for the visit and Beale read out the warrant. On hearing these words Mary crossed herself and said this was welcome news, 'for it announces the termination of my miseries, and the grace which God has vouchsafed me that I die for the honour of his name and his church. I did not, expect such a happy end, after the treatment I have suffered, and the dangers to which I have been exposed in this country for nineteen years- I who was born a queen, the daughter of a king, the (great) grand-daughter of Henry VII, the near kinswomen of the Queen of England, Queen-Dowager of France- and who, though a free princess, have been kept in prison without lawful cause, though I am subject to nobody, and recognise no superior on earth but God.'

Mary laid her hand on the New Testament on her table and declared she was innocent of being part of a conspiracy to kill Elizabeth, and the Earl of Kent responded that the bible in which she swore on was of the Church of Rome and her oath was of no value. Mary asked if swearing on a Protestant bible would be acceptable to the Earl of Kent, and whether it would matter that she did not believe in that version. She also asked that she be allowed a priest which was refused although the Earl of Kent offered the Protestant Dean of Peterborough, which Mary declined with astonishment.

One of Mary's household was Pierre de Bourdeille, seigneur de Brantome who was a French noble. He would write about the events on the day of the execution; an account which would be first published in 1665, *The Execution of Mary, Queen of Scots, 1587.*

When Mary asked when she was to be executed the Earl of Shrewsbury told her 8 o'clock, tomorrow morning. Mary asked for more time to make final arrangements and write out her will, of which the Earl of Shrewsbury responded harshly: 'No, no, Madam you must die, you must die! Be ready between seven and eight in the morning. It cannot be delayed a moment beyond that time.'

Mary would spend the remainder of the day and night composing letters to her friends, relatives and supporters, there were tearful and emotional farewells to her ladies.

"The scaffold had been erected in the middle of a large room. It measured twelve feet along each side and two feet in height, and was covered by a coarse cloth of linen. The Queen entered the room full of grace and majesty, just as if she were coming to a ball. There was no change on her features as she entered. Drawing up before the scaffold, she summoned her major-domo and said to him:

'Please help me mount this. This is the last request I shall make of you.'

Then she repeated to him all that she had said to him in her room about what he should tell her son. Standing on the scaffold, she asked for her almoner, (chaplain) begging the officers present to allow him to come. But this was refused point-blank. The Earl of Kent told her that he pitied her greatly to see her thus the victim of the superstition of past ages, advising her to carry the cross of Christ in her heart rather than in her hand. To this she replied that it would be difficult to hold a thing so lovely in her hand and not feel it thrill the heart, and that what became every Christian in the hour of death was to bear with him the true Symbol of Redemption."

Once Mary stood on the scaffold, Mary would reject further offers of the service of a Protestant minister. She would kneel and ask that her ladies-in-waiting are spared punishment. She would also pray for the conversion of Britain and Scotland to the Catholic Church.

"When this was over, she summoned her women to help her remove her black veil, her head-dress, and other ornaments. When the executioner attempted to do this, she cried out:

'Nay, my good man, touch me not!'

But she could not prevent him from touching her, for when her dress was lowered as far as her waist; the scoundrel caught her roughly by the arm and pulled off her doublet. Her skirt was cut so low that her neck and throat, whiter than alabaster, were revealed. She concealed these as well as she could, saying that she was not used to disrobing in public, especially before so large an assemblage. There were about four or five hundred people present.

The executioner fell to his knees before her and implored her forgiveness. The Queen told him that she willingly forgave him and all who were responsible for her death, as freely as she hoped her sins would be forgiven by God. Turning to the woman to whom she, had given her handkerchief, she asked for it.

She wore a golden crucifix, made out of the wood of the true cross, with a picture of Our Lord on it. She was about to give this to one of her women, but the executioner forbade it, even though Her Majesty had promised that the woman would give him thrice its value in money.

After kissing her women once more, she bade them go, with her blessing, as she made the sign of the cross over them. One of them was unable to keep from crying, so that the Queen had to impose silence upon her by saying she had promised that nothing of the kind would interfere with the business in hand. They were to stand back quietly, pray to God for her soul, and bear truthful testimony that she had died in the bosom of the Holy Catholic religion.

One of the women then tied the handkerchief over her eyes. The Queen quickly, and with great courage, knelt down, showing no signs of faltering. So great was her bravery that all present were moved, and there were few among them that could refrain from tears. In their hearts they condemned themselves for the injustice that was being done.

The executioner, or rather the minister of Satan, strove to kill not only her body but also her soul, and kept interrupting her prayers. The Queen repeated in Latin the Psalm beginning, *In te, Damine, speravi; nan canfundar in aeternum.* When she was through she laid her head on the block, and as she repeated the prayer, the executioner struck her a great blow upon the neck, which was not, however, entirely severed. Then he struck twice more, since it was obvious that he wished to make the victim's martyrdom all the more severe. It was not so much the suffering, but the cause, that made the martyr.

The executioner then picked up the severed head and, showing it to those present, cried out: 'God save Queen Elizabeth! May all the enemies of the true Evangel thus perish!'

Saying this, he stripped off the dead Queen's head-dress, in order to show her hair, which was now white, and which she had been afraid to show to everyone when she was still alive, or to have properly dressed, as she did when her hair was fair and light.

It was not old age that had turned it white, for she was only thirty-five when this took place and scarcely forty when she met her death, but the troubles, misfortunes, and sorrows which she had suffered, especially in her prison." (Bourdeille)

The Earl of Kent would approach the dead body of Mary and declare, 'So perish all the queen's and the gospel's enemies!'

The body lay under a black cloth, to await transportation to the state-room for embalming. Mary's small dog was discovered hiding under the black cloth having sneaked into the hall. By force the loyal dog was forced away from its mistress, covered with blood having lain between head and body.

Once the gates of the castle were opened, the Earl of Shrewsbury's son Henry Talbot was sent to London to inform Elizabeth of the execution. When the Queen of England finally learned of her rival's demise she reportedly went through a series of emotions; regret, anger; she then insisted that she had not ordered this, and would blame Davison her secretary and the Privy Council. Davison would be arrested, thrown in the Tower of London and subjected to a trial before the Star Chamber. He would be demoted from secretary and punished with a fine of £10,000 that left him in poverty for the remainder of his life. As London and England celebrated with bonfires and the ringing of bells, Elizabeth sought to divert the accusations of international princes by claiming that the death warrant she had signed had been conveyed to the Lord-Chancellor without her permission and that she meant to keep it at hand in case of foreign invasion, and the actions of the privy Council in sending the execution order to Fotheringay was also without her approval. She also vented spite towards her councillors, Lord Burleigh was pushed from court, and Walsingham was also targeted although he used the excuse of having been ill during the process of the execution. The Earl of Leicester along with Hatton would be absent from her side for a time.

Overall she was aware that there would be a great deal of hostility from Spain, France and the Vatican in regards to this act, and as for Scotland she would endeavour to find a means to appease the son of the executed mother. One act was to have Mary buried with royal honours in Peterborough Cathedral

After the Execution

King James of Scotland would first hear about the February 8th death of his mother around seven days after, when Robert Ashton, a gentleman of his bedchamber arrived at Edinburgh having spent a short time in London. Elizabeth would also send Sir Robert Carey, the son of her cousin Lord Hunsdon to Scotland. He had in his possession a letter from Elizabeth dated February 14th, but as he reached Berwick requesting a safe-conduct he was ordered by James not to proceed any further. Robert Carlyle, a confidant of Archibald Douglas would write that James would not meet any ambassadors because of 'heaviness and sorrowing of his mother, and also because he is not resolved that the Queen is so sorry for his mother's death as he was informed she was'. Sir Robert Melville and the Laird of Cowdenknowes would meet with Carey and receive the letter as well as a written message from Carey dated March 14th and outlining a defence of Elizabeth's actions in regards to the execution of Mary. Carey would explain that Elizabeth had not intended to put Mary to death, despite the pressure from council, parliament and the 'poor people and commonality.' She signed the death warrant as a last resort in the event of invasion from France and Spain, and many reports would be received in regards to such fears. She handed the death warrant to Davison with the intention he keep it secret and only pass it to the council if there is an attempt against herself or a threat to England, and there they would act under their own discretion. Davison however showed it to several councillors who in turn assembled the whole council who would rule that Mary should be immediately executed. Elizabeth would claim that she knew nothing of these proceedings until it was too late. She would send Davison to the Tower of London on February 14th; he would later be tried by the Star Chamber, imprisoned and fined the sum of £10,000. The English secretary Francis Walsingham would write to Archibald Douglas that Elizabeth 'is violently bent against Mr. Davison, which seemeth to proceed of a desire she hath thereby to satisfy the King his sovereign. Would there were some better course of satisfaction taken'. Walsingham was perhaps of the opinion that the prosecution of Davison was disingenuous.

When Sir Robert Melville and Cowdenknowes returned to Edinburgh and showed James the letters, he would read the handwritten words of Elizabeth which were expressed in sadness and regret. 'Dear Brother, I would you knew, though I would not have you feel, my extreme grief for 'that miserable accident which far contrary to my meaning has befallen.' I now send my kinsman to inform you of the truth. God and men know that I am innocent. If I had 'bidden do it I would have abided by it.' Fear of living men would not drive me to do what is unjust; nor to deny what I have done. If I had meant to do this deed, I would not lay the blame on others; nor will I condemn myself, since I am innocent of it. As for yourself, believe me that you have not a more loving kinswomen, nor a dearer friend, than myself in all the world.' These are affectionate words although there may have been a large measure of realpolitik as England was under threat from Spain and a war with Scotland would place England at a severe disadvantage

We have no record of how James reacted to this letter from Elizabeth; he may have been touched by the words of sorrow, and most importantly of the commitment to friendship. He would need to balance his own ambition for the English succession with the growing anger that would begin to emerge when the news of the execution spread. There were also placards posted in the streets condemning James, Archibald Douglas, the Master of Gray and the Protestant preachers of supporting and conniving in the execution of Mary. There were also 'very odious and detestable' libels produced against the Queen of England. On the borders men like Lord Maxwell, Kerr of Ancrum and Kerr of Ferniehurst were threatening to cross the border and were awaiting the word from the king. James would summon these warlike men to Holyrood Palace for several days, and whilst he convinced them that he thirsted for revenge his true plan was to keep them from provoking war with England. Claude Hamilton and Lord Arbroath promised to raise 3,000 men, and the Earl of Bothwell declared that his suit of armour would be his mourning garment.

Whilst James would openly express anger as his nobles and the people cried out for vengeance, it was also believed that his heart experienced joy at the news. His secretary Maitland was careful that no visitors should witness this joy yet it was recorded that on the night of the news James would declare triumphantly, 'I am now sole King!' As the news became known over the next few weeks, the satisfaction of James would be observed by others. However Sir Robert Melville's brother James Melville the diarist, would write that the king sought revenge, although he may have being witnessing what may have been an example of the charade James played out to appease his angry nobility.

The French secretary in Scotland, Courcelles, did not believe that James would react violently against England; his claims to the English throne were too much a goal to throw it away with a war of revenge. Nevertheless James would assemble a convention of the estates to discuss and determine which direction the Scots should take. During this period, where James was under pressure from Catholic lords of the north and the borderers wanting war, he would manage to frustrate and delay any actions that would threaten the Anglo-Scot treaty. He would have been influenced by a letter that the secretary John Maitland had received from Francis Walsingham which outlined the reasons why James should not go to war. Dated March 4th it is an example of cold logical thinking. Walsingham would claim he was not present at court when Mary was executed, and having spoke with Archibald Douglas he was now concerned about reports that 'the Queen's death is likely' to alienate James 'and move him to revenge.'

Walsingham would make several points on why James should not pursue a 'war of revenge' as the execution 'was a act of necessity' and 'full of so honourable and just proceedings.' He would declare that England, 'strong in the support of the God of Justice, need not fear the issue.' He would also add that Scotland did not have the resources or 'strength to stand against the might of England.' He warned against allying with France and Spain, questioning the reliability of such princes, whilst England was strong and could call on Dutch sea power to counter any foreign invasion. There was also the question of James's religion, and Henri III of France would oppose the prospect of a Protestant king uniting Scotland, England, Wales and Ireland, and as James was a relative of the Guise family, his rivals for power, he believed that the King of France would deem it 'unsafe to promote the cause of their kinsman'. Any French support would be to cause a 'war of diversion' which would result in 'the effusion of much Scottish blood for French quarrels. Seeking Spanish support may renew Philip II's claims to the throne of England through blood ties to the

House of Lancaster and through a donation from James's mother. Even if James changed his religion to win over France and Spain, many of the English Catholics would doubt his sincerity and Protestants would unite against him as an apostate. Walsingham wrote of the possible consequences, if James should be slain, captured or chased into exile. He also warned that the English people would not choose a prince as king if he preferred the friendship of England's enemies, and those judges, nobles and gentlemen who had ruled for execution would be assured opponents of James as they would naturally fear a 'vindictive ruler, who would doubtless one day proceed against them.'

The English secretary would commend the king for his efforts to save his mother's life through mediation, and assured that this would not alienate the nobility and common as they understood his actions were 'natural as long as hope remained', now though they expected him not to express 'true honour' through 'passion or fury' but to act 'within the compass of decency and justice.' They would expect to James to 'end sorrowing' and accept her death, and Walsingham expressed his own 'desire' for the 'continuance of amity between the two crowns' for the 'common well of the whole island.'

James when faced with these words would need to face up to the dire consequences of a war with England, which Walsingham astutely explained would lose him the English succession. The best and most logical course for James was to continue the peace with Elizabeth and England, and in time he would win the crown of England.

In the months that followed James managed to play the angered son, yet managed to ensure that there was no break in relations between Scotland and England, and whilst there would be raids across the border by Scots in vengeful mood, it was not enough to cause war. By following this course James was ably supported and advised by Maitland.

By the summer James would reach his maturity and thoughts were diverted to marriage and finding a queen.

The Fates of Gray and Douglas

After the death of Mary, there would be widespread condemnation against King James, the Master of Gray, and Archibald Douglas. Gray would also be temporarily ostracised by Francis Walsingham the English secretary, who would complain to Archibald Douglas that he cannot 'find in his heart to write' to him due to his 'ill dealing' which may have been a allusion to the suspicions that Gray was acting on behalf of the French during the recent embassy.

Archibald Douglas would discover through many sources including Sir Robert Melville, that 'you lack not unfriends' in Scotland, a unique Scottish term describing enemies. Melville would decline a request to act as Douglas's friend, explaining that 'it is hard for the present to any friend to satisfy all speeches, the people here are so inflamed.' Douglas's nephew Richard Douglas in a letter dated March 23rd, would relate how he attempted to bring a reconciliation with John Maitland, the secretary of state, only to be met with protests that 'in no manner would he credit with you (Archibald Douglas), but so far as his master would command him, and to deal with you, whom he esteemed his unfriend, and to have done such evil offices for the King, as ye are unworthy to live'. Richard would also write that Maitland would complain that 'ye had been the only cause of this late execution, together with a long commemoration of evil offices done against himself'. Maitland would accuse Archibald Douglas of having called him a 'passionate fool' to the English Council and having presented a 'forged bond' which was claimed was given to the Earl of Arran. Richard Douglas would defend his uncle by stating the fact that he could not have altered the opinion of the whole English council who sought Mary's death, yet despite his efforts he could find no one of power or influence who would act as Archibald's friend in Scotland.

During this period, James's former favourite James Stuart, the Earl of Arran would try and find a way back to court. He would send a letter during March 1587 accusing both the Master of Gray and Maitland of being accomplices in the death of Mary. He also accused Maitland and the former banished lords of having planned to abduct James and hand him over to England.

A hearing was scheduled for April 10th with Arran ordered by the Privy Council to enter himself into ward; refusing this condition the charges were dropped. However, Arran's brother Sir William Stuart of Monkton had befriended the Master of Gray. Stuart had been requested by James on March 26th to travel to France. Stuart would learn more about Gray's doings over the past few years, and revealed all to the king. At a convention at Holyrood commenced on May 10th, he accused Gray of being an accomplice in the coup of November 1585 which brought the fall of his brother James Stuart, Earl of Arran. He also accused 'Sir John Maitland of Thirlestane, knight, secretary, Andrew Wood of Largo, comptroller, Sir John Bellenden of Auchnoull, knight, justice clerk, Walter Stuart, prior of Blantyre, keeper of the privy seal, and William Keith, master of his highness's wardrobe', of being 'art, part and upon the foreknowledge of the raid'. Several persons involved in that aforementioned raid, who had already been pardoned for their part; John Hamilton, Lord Arbroath, Francis Stuart, Earl of Bothwell, John Erskine, Earl of Mar, Lord Hailes and others would swear by oath that none of the above accused by Captain Stuart was involved in conspiring or planning the raid of Stirling. King James upon hearing their testimonies absolved

Gray and the others and declared that 'every one of them to be honest, faithful, true, and to have behaved themselves in all things towards his majesty to his highness's honour, contentment and satisfaction.'

Maitland also received word that he was the subject of assassination plot by Gray, in which he, Sir James Home of Cowdenknowes, and Mr Robert Douglas, provost of Lincluden, were to be abducted by Captain William Stuart with the support of John Maxwell, Earl of Morton, which would be followed by the return of James Stuart, Earl of Arran. He would make a complaint against Gray before the Holyrood Convention on May 15th, which would be confirmed by Captain Stuart. Gray denied the accusations, or of having ever had such a conversation with Stuart. The latter retorted by attacking Gray's reputation, reminding all that having been tasked as an ambassador to save the King's mother, he instead conspired to have her executed, having quoted in a letter to Elizabeth the Latin motto *Mortui non mordent*, the dead don't bite, which he was accused of having written the previous summer 1586. The Council ordered that a trial be set for May 23rd and both Gray and Stuart were warded in Edinburgh castle.

When the trial commenced, comprising senators, the council, and the criminal justice, Stuart repeated his accusations, and also added further information that Gray had requested that when he travelled to France he contact certain Catholic spies, the Jesuit James Tyrie, Friar Gray, and Charles Neville, Earl of Westmoreland, and then use them as intermediaries with both the pope and King Philip of Spain, and from that point request the Spanish and Papal ambassadors and agents to communicate with both the Henry, Duke of Guise and Henry III, King of France, informing them that James may seek their aid in revenging the death of his mother, and advising that they set a condition that in return for aid he introduce liberty of conscience for Catholics in Scotland.

The Master of Gray noting that he would receive no favour from the King, and also being secretly informed that admitting these charges would invite mercy, confessed 'himself culpable in presence of them all, while he wished rather to be imputed by the imperfection of youth and ambition, where unto he is somewhat addicted, rather than any malicious enterprise; and therefore referred himself over in the king's mercy to dispose upon him as best should please his majesty.' He also admitted writing a letter to Queen Elizabeth on August 1586 recommending she execute Mary for her own security, and that knowing the English were determined to do so he suggested it be done in a private manner and not public. It appears that Gray's old associate Leicester may have leaked details of this letter to the Scots. Whilst he admitted acting against Mary during the summer 1586, there was no evidence presented that he had acted treacherously during his 1586/87 embassy to England, and all indications press the case that he did act to save Mary's life. He may have also been recruited into the French camp as was suspected by the English, and Leicester's leaking of the incriminating letter to Elizabeth may have been an act of retaliation. Gray would also admit stirring up rebellion in Scotland, of conspiring with French interests for the cause of liberty of conscience, and of using counterfeit stamps and letters in falsifying the King's authority. He would also add that he was also conspiring to hinder any marriage proposals between James and Princess Anne, daughter of the King of Denmark, for the reason that Denmark was Protestant and such a marriage would 'disturb the intentions and travails of the said master and his accomplices' in bringing liberty of conscience to Scotland.

Gray having admitted treason on several counts should have been given the harshest sentences, yet he would avoid execution when John Hamilton, Lord Arbroath, who owed a debt to him, would intercede on his behalf. James would support Lord Arbroath's petition as did seemingly the bulk of the estates. The criminal justice would order that Gray pass over the Firth of Forth where he may settle his family and business affairs, and within a month he was to be banished from Scotland. This was proclaimed in Edinburgh on June 26th and carried throughout the realm.

On July 1587 the Master of Gray would travel to France where he served as a mercenary soldier. John Maitland of Thirlestane would be ratified as chancellor of Scotland at the July parliamentary session. For Archibald Douglas his fortunes would change when he was instructed by the King, through Richard Douglas, to lobby Queen Elizabeth to be named second person and heir apparent to England, and if she refuses at least to write a letter acknowledging the King's rights and claims. He also sought that Elizabeth grant him lands in northern England and give him the title Duke. He also wanted to have a veto in regards to any marriage plans of Arabella Stuart his nearest rival to the throne.

The mission assigned to Archibald Douglas met with no success and he was said to have been dismissed as ambassador in England in 1587. Nevertheless he would retain a role as unofficial ambassador based in London living in a house at Lime Street, and James would be forced to write to Elizabeth in June 1589 to complain that Douglas did not have the commission to act in his name.

The League between England and Scotland which both sought to preserve, was tested in 1588, the year of the Spanish Armada, when

Philip of Spain prepared to send several hundred ships to England to invade and conquer. James showed his commitment to the League when during May he led an army into Dumfriesshire to drive out Lord Maxwell, recently deprived of his earldom of Morton, and Colonel William Stuart, both of which were preparing to raise troops to support the Spanish invasion.

The Master of Gray would return to Scotland soon after this expedition. There is little known about Gray's mercenary career in France, likely he joined Sir James Colville of Easter Wemyss, an officer in who brought Scots soldiers to support Henry of Navarre. It is said that Gray believed serving as a mercenary would not be a good long-term career move and decided to once more try his luck in Scotland. His rift was Francis Walsingham was healed and on May 31st 1588 he arrived in Scotland. Walsingham had sent James Hudson to Scotland to vouch for Gray and try to reconcile him with Maitland, and Gray himself would bring letters of credit from Elizabeth and a commission to look after 'her majesty's affairs in Scotland'. He was soon afterwards made a privy councillor and master of the royal wardrobe. Elizabeth was interested in the progress of marriage negotiations that James sought with princess Anne of Denmark, and obviously she wanted a friendly voice in James's council although Gray would no longer enjoy his former influence. Elizabeth would also want a friendly Scotland in respect to the threat of the Spanish Armada.

In June the Armada would leave the Spanish seaports for England, 130 ships strong, carrying 22,000 troops, and 8,000 sailors. Fearing that northern Scotland may be a destination, the whole country was mobilised in preparation, bales being lit on top of hills and the cause and defence of religion used as a rallying cry. From July 21st to July 29th the Armada reeled under the resolute attacks of the English navy, and hampered by heavy gales dispersed and blown west beyond Ireland, and then north past Scotland. The gales drove many ships to shipwreck on the coasts, and left the Spanish subject to the mercy of the inhabitants. The survivors would make their way past the east coast of Scotland and to the haven of the ports on mainland Europe. James would be pleased with the part he had played in suppressing support for Spain within Scotland, proving his commitment to the League.

James could now concentrate on concluding marriage negotiations with the royal house of Denmark. On August 20th 1589 the George Keith, Earl Marshall of Scotland would take part in a proxy marriage with the sixteen year old Anne, where he took the place of James. The adverse weather would prevent Anne from travelling to Scotland and instead James would with kingly chivalry travel to Norway in October 1589 with 300 personal, arriving back at Leith on May 1st with the new Queen of Scotland. On May 17th, a Sunday, Anne would be crowned in the Abbey Kirk of Holyrood, the ceremony performed by the Edinburgh minister Robert Bruce.

Archibald Douglas would continue to play the role of unofficial ambassador to Scots in England, retaining an influence with the English court and council. He would support his stepson Francis Stuart, Earl of Bothwell when he was exiled from Scotland for various offences including a charge in April 1591 of using witches to raise storms to hazard the journey of James and Anne from Norway. In 1592 he conducted a failed attempt on June 28th to abduct King James during the Raid of Falkland Palace, where he had been joined by Colonel Stuart, the Earls of Errol and Angus, the lairds of Johnson and Balweary, and the

Master of Gray. Feeling himself sidelined by James through the influence of Maitland of Thirlestane, Gray had joined the rebels in an attempt to regain some influence. Bothwell was chased over the border, and enjoyed some favour in England during his exile. His fellow conspirators were not vigorously punished, the Earl of Errol and Colonel were briefly imprisoned and released after no proofs were produced. Other courtiers implicated in the plot went through the procedures of examination before being restored to favour. The Master of Gray would try to win the favour of James by accusing the influential Edinburgh minister Robert Bruce of being part of the plot, and asked the exiled Bothwell to back his claims. Bothwell, not trusting Gray, declined to get involved. At the trial Gray denied making the accusation and offered to fight anybody exempting the king, who would claim he accused Bruce. The matter was dropped with no evidence produced. Gray's reputation would be damaged although he would in 1593 be granted a remission for his part in the failed Falkland Raid. From then on he appeared to steer away from plots of significance, continuing as a privy councillor, as well as master of the wardrobe and hereditary sheriff of Angus. He would be given permission to travel to Europe in 1596, and when he returned he would offer his services to Sir Robert Cecil, Secretary of State for England and son of William, Lord Burghley. The offer was refused. After the death of his father Lord Gray in March 10th, 1608, the Master would come into his inheritance and become Patrick, 6th Lord Gray. He would die a few years later on September 4th 1611.

In late 1592, Captain James Stuart the former Earl of Arran would see the political upheavals as an opportunity to return to royal favour. Having been residing in the west he would be ambushed by James Douglas of

Parkhead, nephew of the executed James Douglas, 4th Earl of Morton. He would be sliced to pieces, his head placed on a pike and carried before the revenged Douglas clan. Archibald Douglas would no doubt be pleased with this news, an avowed enemy slain. He would continue to be an individual who would involve himself in several plots over the years. He would continue to act as go-between between Bothwell and the English court during his stepson's subsequent plots to gain possession of James and the Scottish government. When Bothwell was chased out of Scotland on 1594 after another attempt to possess the king, Elizabeth was sent a letter by James chastening her for apparently supporting the exiled Earl. Elizabeth agreed to end giving Bothwell refuge, and he would leave for France.

Archibald Douglas would be deposed by the General Assembly of Scotland from the post of parson of Douglas and Glasgow through non-attendance on March 1593, cutting him off from vital sources of finance and information. Resident in a house in Lime Street, London he would still be approached in various schemes and plots, whether from Catholic Earls in Scotland, or from Spanish agents seeking to invade England or Ireland. The date of his death is not known although he is recorded to be alive in the summer of 1602, 'unfit for ony service; and with a urge to return to Scotland.'

Patrick, Master of Gray and Archibald Douglas are examples of professional diplomats, highly educated, with astute personal qualities and charms, who possessed the skills to insert themselves into the circles of power and manipulate events for an employee or for their own advantage. Most importantly they were able to create networks across borders and seas, where communication was through letters, often encrypted messages. It was these networks that made Gray and Douglas important player in politics, they provided information and news, they served as channels for spies and informers, and anyone with political ambitions would need to consider whether to bring these people into their plans, or consider the possible consequences if they did not. This would explain how Gray and Douglas were able to switch sides so easily, they were basically in the market not just to sell their skills but also lease out the use of their networks. Gray's career leading up to the execution of Mary, Queen of Scots is a dizzying example of intrigues and personal ambition. Winning the confidence of the Guise family in France, he wins the confidence of Mary. He then betrays the French, offers his services to the English, and then intrigues to bring the downfall of James Stuart, Earl of Arran in what was an example of a genius coup d' etat. He would admit that in August 1586 after the discovery of the Babington Plot, that he suggested to Elizabeth in writing that she have Mary killed, with the logic that 'the dead don't bite'. Within the space of a few months he may have switched from being an English partisan to being recruited by the French, for during the embassy of 1586/87 to England to plead for Mary's life, the record shows that he was vigorous in her defence. His religion was also a mystery, and whilst he was educated in the Protestant environment of St Andrews, he was widely suspected of being a secret Catholic through association with the Guise family, as well as knowing many Jesuits. However this ambiguousness may have suited him, allowing him to fish secrets from both camps.

In regards to Mary's execution Archibald Douglas was following the opinion of the English council and House of Commons who sought her death. He was pragmatic enough to realise that he alone could not change the minds of such institutions, so he worked to convince the English that James would do nothing in retaliation, and he was helped in this attitude by Alexander Stuart of Scotstounhill who would openly claim to know that James would do nothing. The only problem was the attitude of the Scottish ambassadors such as William Keith and Robert Melville, who could push so hard for Mary's life that they may endanger the treaty between Scotland and England. Archibald was also in a situation where he was being blamed for conspiring to have Mary executed, which would make his return to Scotland difficult, so he had no choice but to ensure that he work with the English and stay in England. It also meant that the quicker that Mary was executed the quicker that Scotland and England would negotiate the aftermath. As it happened, James was more concerned with ensuring his place in the succession that pursuing a war of revenge. It was a hard lesson in realpolitik yet James passed, with a loss of honour perhaps although the greater prize was now in sight.

On March 21st 1603, Queen Elizabeth would die, and Sir Robert Carey would arrive at Holyrood on March 24th with the news. On March 26th the Privy Councillors of England would proclaim James Elizabeth's successor and the new monarch. For James the long wait was over, and there was no opposition to this succession, even from his competitor Lady Arabella Stuart. On April 3rd, a Sunday, as James made preparations to travel to England he made a statement to his people; 'Think not of me as a King going from one part to another; but as a King lawfully called, going from one part of the isle to the other, that so your comfort may be greater. And where I thought to employed you with some armour, now I employ only your hearts to the good prospering of me in my success and journey.' James left for his journey on April 5th arriving at Berwick the same day.

He travelled at a slow pace southwards, meeting the people, courting public opinion as he went. James would have his coronation at Westminster on July 25th, where he would be recognised as King James I of England. He and Anne would also produce heirs for the Stuart succession; Henry, Charles and Elizabeth.

James would make a promise to return to Scotland every three years, however during his twenty-two years of ruling England he would visit only once. Scotland had been the stepping stone to the larger and more prosperous kingdom of England, his presence was no longer needed and he would govern his northern kingdom with pen and paper. The death of Mary his mother had cleared the path to the English succession, yet in later life he may have been filled with some regret as in 1612 James would have Mary's body brought from Peterborough Cathedral and reburied at Westminster Abbey alongside Elizabeth. He would also have Fotheringay Castle demolished. There is a plaque at the site where the castle once stood, which reads, 'In memory of Mary Stuart, Queen of Scots, beheaded in the great hall of Fotheringay Castle 8th February 1587 This memorial was placed here by the Stuart History Society in 1964.'

Appendix: The Trial of Patrick, Master of Gray

The following parliamentary records have been translated from the original vernacular. They are copied from The Records of the Parliaments of Scotland to 1707. www.rps.ac.uk/, Reign of James VI, May, 10th, May 15th, 1587.

Procedure: trial of Patrick, master of Gray and others for the raid at Stirling Castle

The which day, in presence of the king's majesty, his nobility, council and estates presently convened, Sir William Stewart [of Monkton], brother german to [James Stewart, earl of Arran], late chancellor, declared and affirmed that Patrick [Gray], master of Gray, confessed and declared to him of late, amongst his other speeches, that he, together with Sir John Maitland of Thirlestane, knight, secretary, Andrew Wood of Largo, comptroller, Sir John Bellenden of Auchnoull, knight, justice clerk, Walter [Stewart], prior of Blantyre, keeper of the privy seal, and William Keith, master of his highness's wardrobe, were art, part and upon the foreknowledge of the raid and incoming of the noblemen and others at Stirling in the month of November the year of God 1585. Which persons, being personally present and hearing the said declaration and affirmation, touching them most highly in honour and duty, craved and desired most humbly of his majesty, his said nobility and estates, least they or any others should be persuaded that the same in any way was true, that they might be presently tried, and to that effect that the oaths and declaration of the noblemen and others presently convened who repaired to Stirling at the time foresaid, together with the said Patrick, master of Gray, alleged speaker thereof, might be presently taken, through which their innocency or guiltiness might be known and order taken with them as appertained. The king's majesty, his said nobility, council and estates, finding the desire of the foresaid persons to be very reasonable, required John [Hamilton], lord Hamilton, Francis [Stewart], earl of Bothwell, lord Hailes, Crichton and Liddesdale, John [Erskine], earl of Mar, lord Erskine, and certain others who came to Stirling at the time foresaid, to declare the truth; and they, being all sworn, declared by their great oaths that the foresaid persons were in no way art, part nor upon the foreknowledge of their coming to Stirling, neither had they nor any of them, nor no others being with them in company, so far as they knew, any intelligence with them by letters, messages nor no other manner of way, directly nor indirectly, at any time before they were received to his majesty's favour. Likewise the said Patrick, master of Gray, being also sworn, testified that he at no time made any such confession or declaration to the said Sir William as he presently affirms, neither did he know of any such form of doing to have been used by the said persons or any of them, but that they behaved themselves as honest, faithful and true to his majesty in this and all other things, as become them of duty; and farther, that he spoke not of having any letter of the said Walter, prior of Blantyre, in a black box, that would disgrace him at his highness's hands, as the said Sir William likewise affirmed, neither had he any letter of the said prior's sent to him at any time, saving one direct missive, advertising him of some ill-will and malice borne to him by the late chancellor, proceeding, as he then and yet does suppose, of a goodwill towards him, and that he would not at any time have wished any inconvenience to have fallen out beside his majesty. With the which declarations made by the said noblemen and others foresaid, his highness being well and sufficiently satisfied, has esteemed, and presently and in all times hereafter wills and does esteem, the foresaid persons and every one of them to be honest, faithful, true, and to have behaved themselves in all things towards his majesty to his highness's honour, contentment and satisfaction.

Procedure: accusations against Patrick, master of Gray for the raid at Stirling Castle

The which day Patrick [Gray], master of Gray, commendator of Dunfermline, compeering in presence of the king's majesty, his nobility and estates assembled at this present convention, and Sir William Stewart [of Monkland], lawful son to Andrew [Stewart], lord Stewart of Ochiltree, compeering also personally, they having been brought face to face before in presence of his majesty and his privy council upon the occasion of the dilation and accusation following, and thereafter both committed to ward within the castle of Edinburgh until this present convention of the said estates, the said Sir William, now as of before, accused the said Master of Gray how he, within this year bypast, had dealt and travailed in France for sundry matters prejudicial to the true religion presently professed by our sovereign lord and his good subjects and established by law, chiefly to have liberty of conscience to use such form of religion as served every man's appetite, contrary to the tenor of the acts of parliament, and to this effect gave great persuasions and special instructions to the said Sir William to deal with certain persons in France, namely Friar Gray, Mr James Tyrie, Jesuit, and [Charles Nevill], earl of Westmorland, banished out of England for religion, and also to have dealt as intermediaries with Pope [Sixtus V] and [Philip II], king of Spain, that their ambassadors or commissioners might have been directed to [Henry III], king of France and [Henri de Lorraine], duke of Guise, willing them to grant no aid to the king of Scotland unless he gave liberty of conscience to all the Catholics in his bounds, for the which travail it was spoken and devised by the said master how the said Sir William should have received sums of money. Item, that the said Master of Gray had travailed in matters which greatly [...] disturbed the estate of the realm, wherein if his travails had taken effect [...] been endangered, committing through this the crime of treason and specially traffick [...] to persuade his majesty [...] as the said master should have persuaded [...] to apply to his treasonable [...] used by the young laird of [...] that ever wished his highness well, honour and standing, in no way minded to be compliant with the plotting of so infamous a person. And seeing that first plot not in appearance effectual, that the said master, all of a sudden, devised the second, namely the death of Sir John Maitland of Thirlestane, knight, his majesty's secretary and vice-chancellor, Sir James Home of Cowdenknowes, knight, captain of the castle of Edinburgh, and Mr Robert Douglas, provost of Lincluden, collector-general, all of his highness's privy council, and that, by earnest persuasion of the said Sir William, to make his brother the late chancellor concur with John [Maxwell], earl of Morton, lord Maxwell, whom the said master affirmed that he had made to that purpose, appointing them to come with the number of eighty horses to Lauder, and there enclose the said councillors in the thatch house wherein they were until they had been compelled to be used according to the cruel appetite of the pursuers, as was devised by the said master, thinking thereby that, so many of his majesty's council being taken away by time, the said master was the more able to bring his schemes to fulfilment concerning the disturbance of religion, his majesty's person and the estate of the realm and commonwealth. Item, that the said master had counterfeit his majesty's stamp in his hands, and especially that the said counterfeit stamp was put by the said master to two letters written with his majesty's own hand, which letters contained credit to the said Sir William to treat in certain matters concerning his highness's honour and the welfare and state of the country; and the same credit the said Sir William was persuaded by the said master to use to another sense altogether, contrary to his majesty's direction, specially willing the said Sir William to persuade the king of France to grant no assistance of men to our sovereign lord at this time, showing that, if men should be sent to Scotland at his highness's desire, it would but trouble the Catholics and malcontents with the estate present, albeit in truth the said master's design in the matter was for the only cause following, namely that the time of his consenting to the death and murder of [Mary], the queen, his majesty's dearest mother, for the sumptuous gratitudes and rewards which the said master had received in England, therefore he was under special bond and condition still to proceed in his former treasonable dealing, and at the uttermost of his possibility to stop and stay his majesty from the aid and concurrence of other foreign princes, and also, if the said Sir William should crave money from the king of France, it would make it all too clear who are enemies and have the handling of this estate presently. Upon which all points the said Master of Gray being separately interrogated and questioned in presence of his majesty and his said nobility and estates, and his answers and allegations heard and understood by them, questions being formed upon the foresaid accusation by the said estates and laid to the charge of the said Master of Gray, he granted the four points following: first, that he had written to the queen of England about the month of August last bypast, without his highness's knowledge or command, bearing in effect that if the queen of England could not perceive her own security in taking his majesty's mother's life, because the dead do not bite, yet it was in no way fit that the same be done openly, but rather by some quieter means; secondly, that he had travailed with some of France to move our said sovereign lord upon necessity to grant liberty of conscience; thirdly, the making and using of his majesty's stamp in manner before rehearsed; and fourthly, that he had travailed for the rebellion and troubling of this present estate; all which four crimes were found by the king's majesty and his said estates to be treasonable and worthy of all highest punishment; and it was found superfluous and needless to lead any further proof against him in this instance; and that therefore the said Sir William, as having only dealt in the matter for our sovereign lord's service, should be set at liberty and merited reward, and the said master, as guilty, to be used according to his majesty's will and pleasure. The said estates most humbly and earnestly making intercession to his majesty for sparing of the said master's life, as also his heritage, upon his good and dutiful behaviour towards his majesty in time coming, which being most graciously and favourably granted by his highness, the said Master of Gray thereafter voluntarily confessed two other points, namely that he had travailed for the alteration and troubling of the present state; the other point following, namely that he had travailed for the staying and hindering of our sovereign lord's marriage with [Anne of Denmark], the king of Demark's daughter, fearing if his highness should ally with any Christian prince professing the said true religion, that it should disturb the intention and travails of the said master and his accomplices, with whom the said Sir William, for the cause above-written, should have dealt. Moreover, his majesty, with advice of the said estates, decrees and declares that, in case the said master or any of his kin, friends, allies or servants, shall presume or attempt any violent deed or invasion against the said Sir William for the causes foresaid, that thereby they shall be similarly culpable of the whole crimes foresaid as the said master himself, and ordains letters to be directed for publication hereof at the market crosses of the head burghs of this realm and other places needful, that none pretend ignorance of the same.

Bibliography.

In writing this work, I followed closely the narratives of the 18th and 19th century historians, William Robertson (The History of Scotland), the Rev. Thomas Thomson (A History of the Scottish People), Thomas Wright (The History of Scotland). Although I didn't always agree with their opinions, good old-fashioned analysis and research was found from Alice Strichland (Lives of the Queens of Scotland), and Patrick Fraser Tytler (History of Scotland).

For contemporary sources; the *Warrender Papers*, vol.1 and vol.2 (Scottish History Society); *Letters and Papers relating to the Master of Gray* (Bannatyne Club), *Memoirs of Sir James Melville of Halhill, 1535-1617* (ed. Francois Stuart), and the *Calendar of State Papers Relating to Scotland and Mary Queen of Scots* (ed. Joseph Bain), were very useful for gaining an insight into the motivations and opinions of the principle characters. *The Calendar of State Papers, Spain,* and *The Calendar of State Papers, Spain (Simancas)*, are useful in that they give the Spanish analysis of events in Scotland and England, and are also filled with information that often can be corroborated.

Primary Sources

AGA. Acts of the General Assemblies, 1560-1583. Edited by Duncan Shaw. The Scottish Record Society. Edinburgh. 2004.

ALHTS. Accounts of the Lord High Treasurer of Scotland. Edited by Sir James Balfour Paul. Vol. 9, 1546-51. Vol. 10, 1551-59. Vol.11, 1559-1566. Edinburgh.

ATS. Accounts of the Treasurer of Scotland. Edited by Charles Thorpe McInnes. Vol. 12, 1566-1574. Edinburgh, 1970.

Bourdeille, Pierre de. (1665), *The Execution of Mary, Queen of Scots, 1587.*

Buchanan, George, The History of Scotland, Edited by James Aitkin. Glasgow, 1827.

Colville, John. Historie of the life of King James the Sext, Being an account of the affairs of Scotland from 1566 to 1596; with a short continuation to 1617. Edited by Rev. Thomas Thomson.

CP. Calender of the Cecil Papers in Hatfield House, vol.1, 1306-1571.

CSPF. Calender of State Papers, Foreign. Edward VI 1547-1553. Mary 1553-1558. Elizabeth 1558-1561.

CSPRS. Calendar of State Papers Relating to Scotland and Mary Queen of Scots, Joseph Bain (ed.). H.M. General, Edinburgh 1898.
CSPS. Calendar of State Papers, Spain, vol. 6-13.
CSPSS. Calendar of State Papers, Spain (Simancas), vol.1.
CSPV. Calendar of State Papers relating to English Affairs in the Archives of Venice, vol. 5-7.
CSPVA. Calendar of State Papers relating to English affairs in the Vatican Archives, vol.1
Diurnnal. A Diurnnal of Remarkable Occurents, Bannatyne Club, 1833.
Donaldson, Gordon (ed.) (1949), The Thirds of Benefices, Scottish History Society, 3rd Series, vol. XLII, Edinburgh.
Dunlop, A. I. (ed.), The Scottish Correspondence of Mary of Lorraine. Scottish History Society, 1927.
ER. Exchequer Rolls of Scotland. Edited by George Powell McNeill. H. M. General Register House, Edinburgh.
ERBE. Extracts from the Records of the Burgh of Edinburgh, 1557-1571, Scottish Burgh Society, Edinburgh 1875.
Herries, Lord, (Historical Memoirs of Reign of Mary…) Abbotsford Club, No.6., 1836.
Holinshed, Ralph. Holinshed's Chronicles of England, Scotland and Ireland (ed.). Vernon, F. S (1965). New York, AMS.
Jooste, Pascale. Translated from the French by Pascale Jooste. The Affairs of the Earl of Bothwell. Castle of Copenhagen, January 5th, 1568.
Knox, John. The Reformation in Scotland. Edited by G. J. Guthrie (1898). The Banner of Truth Trust, Edinburgh and Pennsylvania.
Lesley, John, Bishop of Ross. The History of Scotland (1829). Bannatyne Club, Edinburgh.
Letters and Papers relating to the Master of Gray. Bannatyne Club.
LP. Letters and Papers, Foreign and Domestic, Elizabeth I, 1558-1603. Website- British History Online.
Melville, Sir James. Memoirs of Sir James Melville of Halhill, 1535-1617, Edited, with an introduction by A. Francois Steuart Advocate, London, George Routledge & Sons, Ltd. 1929.
Moysie, David. Memoirs of the Affairs of Scotland. James Denniston (ed.). 1830. Bannatyne Club.
Nau, Claude, Memorials of Mary Stuart, BL Cotton MSS, Rev. Joseph Stevenson (ed.).
Pitcairn, R. Ancient Criminal Trials in Scotland, 3 volumes, Bannatyne Club, Edinburgh.
Pollen, J.H. (ed.), (1901), Papal Negotiations with Mary Queen of Scots, 1561-67, Scottish History Society.

RGSS. The Register of the Great Seal of Scotland, 1546-1580. Edited by John Maitland Thomson, 1984.
RPCS. The Register of the Privy Council of Scotland, vol.1, vol2. Edited by John Hill Burton. H. M. General register House, Edinburgh. 1877.
RP. The Records of the Parliaments of Scotland to 1707. www.rps.ac.uk/
RPSS. The Register of the Privy Seal of Scotland. Vol. 5, parts 1 & 2, 1556-1567. Edited by James Beveridge, Gordon Donaldson. Edinburgh, 1957. Vol. 6, 1567-1574. Edited by Gordon Donaldson. Edinburgh, 1963.
Teulot, A. Pie`ces et documents inédits ou peu connus relatifs a` l'histoire de l'Écosse au XVIe sie`cle, tirés des bibliothe`ques et des archives de France, et publiés pour le Bannatyne Club d'Edimbourg. With facsimiles. (3 volumes.) Paged continuously. Text in French, Latin or Spanish. Contents: t. 1. 1515-1564.--t. 2. 1564-1587.
Warrender Papers. Edited by Annie I. Cameron. Two volumes. Scottish History Society. Edinburgh. 1931, 1932.

Secondary Sources

Anderson, P. D. Robert Stewart, Earl of Orkney, Lord of Shetland, 1533-93. 1982.
Anderson, W. History of France. During the Reigns of Francis II and Charles IX (2 volumes).
The 'Ancient Diocese of Macon';
http://www.newadvent.org/cathen/09507a.htm
Bellesheim, Alphons. History of the Catholic Church of Scotland, vol.3 (4 volumes) Edinburgh.
Benger, Miss, Memoirs of the Life of Mary Queen of Scots. 1823.
Bindoff, S. T. Tudor England. Penguin Books. 1950.
Bingham, Caroline (1979) James VI of Scotland.
Burleigh, J.H.S. A Church history of Scotland, London, 1960.
Calderwood, Mr David. The History of the Kirk of Scotland, vol2 (8 volumes), Edinburgh.
Cameron, Annie I. & Rait, Robert S. King James's Secret; Negotiations between Elizabeth I and James VI, 1922.
Chalmers, George (1818). The Life of Mary, Queen of Scotland, drawn from the State Papers. In two volumes, London.
Coventry, Martin (2008). Castles of the Clan, Goblinshead, Musselburgh, Scotland.
Cunningham. Rev. John. The Church History of Scotland, vol.1 (2 volumes), Edinburgh.
Davison, M. H. Armstrong (1965). The Casket Letters. Vision Press

Limited, London.
Dawson, J. E. A (ed.). Campbell Letters, 1559-1583. Scottish History Society. Edinburgh. 1997.
Doughty, D. W. Library of James Stuart, Earl of Moray, 1531-1570. Innes Review, vol.2, pp. 17-29 (1970).
Feiling, K. A History of England. Book Club Associates, 1970 edition.
Fleming, D. H. Mary Queen of Scots, 2nd edition. Hodder and Stroughton, London.
Forbes, F.A. Leaders of a Forlorn Hope. London, 1922.
Forbes-Leith, William (ed.). Narratives of Scottish Catholics (Bishop Leslie's Narrative), Edinburgh, 1885.
Fraser, A. Mary Queen of Scots. Phoenix, London, 1969.
Fraser. G. M. The Steel Bonnets. Barrie &Jenkins Ltd, 1971.
Fraser, William. The Lennox. Edinburgh: [T. & A. Constable], 1874. With plates, including portraits and facsimiles, and genealogical tables. 2 volumes.
Fraser, William. Memoirs of the Maxwells, Earls of Nithsdale, Lords Maxwell & Herries. By William Fraser. Edinburgh : Privately printed for William Lord Herries, 1873.
Froude, J. A. The Reign of Elizabeth. Two Volumes. J. M. Dent & Sons Ltd, London.
Gatherer, W. A (ed.). The Tyrannous Reign of Mary Stewart. George Buchanan's Account. Translated and edited by W. A. Gatherer. Edinburgh, The University Press, 1958.
Gordon, Rev. J.F.S. Monasticon, vol. 1.
Gore-Brown, Robert. Lord Bothwell. Collins, London, 1937.
Grant, J. Memoirs and adventures of Sir William Kirkcaldy of Grange. W Blackstone & Sons, 1849.
Grub, George, Ecclesiastical History of Scotland, vol. 2 (4 volumes), 1861.
Guy, John. The Life of Mary Queen of Scots. My Heart is my Own. Harper Perennial. London. 2004.
Hallam. The Regent Moray. U. C. Berkeley Libraries.
Herkless & Hannay. The Archbishops of St Andrews, vol.5 (5 volumes), Edinburgh.
Howie, John. The Scots Worthies, 2 volumes. W. R. McPhun, Trongate. 1838.
Hume, David. History of the Race and House of Douglas and Angus.
Hume-Brown, P. History of Scotland, 3 volumes. Cambridge: at the university Press, 1911.
James, W. J. Habsburg and Bourbon, 1494-1789. George G. Harrap &

Co. Ltd. 1969 edition.
Jervise, Andrew. History and traditions of the land of the Lindsays in Angus and the Mearns. Rewritten and corrected by James Gammack. Edinburgh : Sutherland & Knox, 1853.
Johnson, A. H. Europe in the 16th Century, 1494-1598. Rivingtons, London. 1932.
Keith, The Right Rev. Robert. A History of the Affairs of Church and State in Scotland, 3 Volumes (ed. John Parker Lawson, notes and additions).
Lee, M. James Stuart, Earl of Moray, New York (1953).
Lee, M. John Maitland of Thirlestane, Princeton (1959).
Lyon, Rev. C. J. History of St Andrews, vol.1, William Tait, Edinburgh.
MacMahon, Major-General R. H. The Tragedy of Kirk o' Field. Cambridge, 1930.
McCabe, Stuart. Let the Wolves Devour. Mereo Books (2015).
MacCulloch, D. Reformation. Europe's House divided. 1490-1700. Penguin Books. 2004.
McGinnis, Paul J. & Williamson, Arthur H (1995). George Buchanan. The Political Poetry. Scottish History Society, Edinburgh.
Marshall, R. K. John Knox. Birlinn Limited. Edinburgh (2000).
Moffat, Alistair. The Reivers. Birlinn, Edinburgh (2008).
Motley, J. L. The Rise of the Dutch Republic. George Routledge and sons, Limited (1904).
ODNB. Oxford Dictionary of National Bibliography. Oxford University Press (2004).
Omond, George W. T., The Lord Advocates of Scotland, Vol.1, Edinburgh.
Patterson, R, C. My Wound is Deep. A History of the later Anglo-Scots Wars, 1380-1560. John Donald publishers Limited, Edinburgh (1997).
Petrie, C. Philip II of Spain. Readers Union, Eyre & Spottiswoode. London (1964).
Pryde, George S (ed.). Ayr Burgh Accounts 1534-1624, Scottish History Society, 3rd Series, vol. 28, Edinburgh (1937).
Ridley, Jasper. The Freemasons. Constable & Robinson Ltd, London. 1999.
Robertson, William. The History of Scotland, vol.2. London. 1806.
Ross, Rev. William (1885), Aberbour and Inchcolme, Being Historical Notices of the Parish and Monastery, David Douglas, Edinburgh.
SAS, A New Statistical Account of Scotland, 15 volumes. William Blackwood and Sons, Edinburgh & London (1845).
SBSH, A Source Book of Scottish History, 3 volumes. Edited by W.

Croft Dickinson, Gordon Donaldson & Isabel A Milne. Thomas Nelson & Sons Ltd. 1952.
Scott, A (ed.). The Poems of Alexander Scott. The Saltire Society. Oliver & Boyd. 1952.
Scott, Sir Walter, History of Scotland, vol.1-3 (1830). Longman, Rees, Orme, Brown & Green. London.
Scott, Sir Walter. The Abbot, Bradbury, Agnew & Co. London. 1877.
SHD. Scottish History Documents. Edited by Gordon Donaldson. Neil Wilson Publishing, Glasgow. 1974 edition.
Skelton, John. Maitland of Lethington and the Scotland of Mary Stuart. In two volumes. William Blackwood and Sons, Edinburgh and London.
Shire, H. M (ed.). Alexander Montgomerie. A Selection from his songs and poems. The Saltire Society. Oliver & Boyd. 1960.
Somerset-Fry, Peter & Fiona. The History of Scotland. Routledge (1982).
SP. Scots Peerage. 9 volumes. Edited by Sir James Balfour Paul, Edinburgh.
Sommerville, P. Protestant resistance theory.
Spottiswood, History of the Church of Scotland, vol.2 (3 volumes), Edinburgh.
Stavert, M. L (ed.). The Perth Guildry Book, 1452-1601. Scottish Record Society, Edinburgh. 1993.
Steeholm, C. & H. James I of England. Michael Joseph Ltd. 1938.
Stephen, Thomas, The History of the Church of Scotland, vol.1 (4 volumes), London.
Strichland, A. (1851). Lives of the Queens of Scotland, vol.5. Harper & Brothers Publisher, New York.
Taylor, Franck (1895), The Regent Moray: The Stanhope Essay. Oxford.
Thomson, Rev. Thomas. A History of the Scottish People, vol. 2-4. Blackie & Son, Limited.
Torrie, Elizabeth P. D. (ed.). The Gild Court Book of Dunfermline, 1433-1597. SCottish record society, New series 12. Edinburgh, 1986.
Tweedie, David (2006). Rizzio & Mary Queen of Scots. Sutton Publishing Limited.
Tytler, P. F. (1828). History of Scotland, William Tait, Edinburgh.
Walker, Nancy H (1983). Lochleven's Royal Prisoner May Queen of Scots. Kinross.
Wallace, P. G. The Long European Reformation. Palgrave MacMillan. 2004.
Walsh, James, History of the Catholic Church in Scotland.
Walton, Kristen Post (2007). Catholic Queen, Protestant Patriarchy. Mary, Queen of Scots, and the Politics of Gender and Religion. Palgrave

Macmillan, Hampshire.

Weir, Alison. Mary, Queen of Scots and the murder of Lord Darnley. BCA. 2003.

Whitehead, Arthur Whiston. Caspard de Coligny, Admiral of France.

Wright, Thomas. The History of Scotland, vol.1-vol.2. The London Printing and Publishing Company. London and New York.

Yellowlees, M. So Strange a monster as a Jesuite. The Society of Jesus in Sixteenth Century Scotland. House of Lochar, Argyll. 2003.

Zweig, Stefan. Mary Stuart. Pushkin Press, London (2011), 1st published 1935.

Made in the USA
Columbia, SC
16 March 2022